Amplify
Your
BRAND

Mastering Social Media Marketing for Rapid Growth

BY

SETH N. TAYLOR

Disclaimer

The information contained in this book is for general purposes only. While every effort has been made to ensure the accuracy and completeness of the content, the author and publisher make no representations or warranties of any kind, express or implied, about the reliability, suitability, or availability of the information. The use of this book and the information within is solely at the reader's discretion, and the author and publisher shall not be held liable for any loss, damage, or injury arising from its use.

Copyright

© [SETH N. TAYLOR] [2023]

Contents

INTRODUCTION

UNDERSTANDING THE POWER OF SOCIAL MEDIA MARKETING

1.1 The Evolution of Social Media

Social media has undeniably transformed the way we communicate, share information, and connect with others. What started as simple online platforms for people to connect and share their thoughts has evolved into a powerful global phenomenon that influences various aspects of our lives. The evolution of social media has been marked by technological advancements, changing user behaviors, and significant societal impacts.

The journey of social media began in the late 1990s and early 2000s with the emergence of platforms like **SixDegrees.com, Friendster, and MySpace**. These early platforms allowed users to create profiles, connect with friends, and share content. However, their reach and impact were relatively limited compared to what was to come.

The turning point in the evolution of social media came with the launch of Facebook in 2004. Facebook introduced a more user-friendly interface and innovative features that captured the attention of millions of users worldwide. It quickly gained popularity among college students and eventually expanded to include people of all ages. Facebook's success set the stage for the social media revolution and paved the way for other platforms to follow.

One of the key factors driving the evolution of social media has been the rapid advancement of technology. The widespread availability of smartphones and the advent of mobile internet opened up new possibilities for social media platforms. Platforms like **Twitter, Instagram, and Snapchat** emerged, catering to the changing preferences and habits of users. These platforms focused on real-time updates, visual content, and ephemeral messaging, catering to the fast-paced nature of modern life.

Another significant aspect of social media's evolution is the shift from purely personal connections to a blend of personal and professional networking. Platforms like LinkedIn gained prominence as a means for professionals to connect, share industry insights, and explore job opportunities. The integration of social media into various industries, such as marketing, journalism, and entertainment, further transformed the way businesses and individuals interact and collaborate.

Moreover, the evolution of social media has also brought attention to the impact it has on society. Social media has become a powerful tool for social movements, activism, and political campaigns. It has enabled individuals to raise awareness about important issues, mobilize communities, and amplify their voices. However, it has also raised concerns about privacy, online harassment, and the spread of misinformation. The influence of social media on mental health and well-being has also garnered significant attention, with studies highlighting both positive and negative effects.

In recent years, the evolution of social media has seen an increased focus on user privacy and data protection. Concerns about data breaches and misuse of personal information have prompted platforms to enhance security measures and give users more control over their data. Regulations and policies regarding social media practices have been implemented in various countries to ensure transparency and accountability.

Looking ahead, the evolution of social media is likely to continue as technology advances and user preferences evolve. Emerging technologies like virtual reality, augmented reality, and artificial intelligence are expected to shape the future of social media, offering new ways to interact and engage with others. Social media platforms will continue to adapt to the changing needs of their users and strive to strike a balance between innovation, user experience, and ethical considerations.

In conclusion, the evolution of social media has been a remarkable journey, transforming the way we communicate, share information, and connect with others. From the early days of simple online profiles to the sophisticated platforms we have today, social media has become an integral part of our daily lives. While it has brought numerous benefits, it also presents challenges and raises important questions about its impact on society. As we move forward, it is crucial to navigate the evolving landscape of social media responsibly and harness its potential for positive change.

1.2 Importance of Social Media Marketing for Brands

Social media has become an integral part of our daily lives, with billions of people actively using various platforms to connect, share, and engage with others. It is no surprise that businesses have recognized the importance of social media marketing as a powerful tool to reach and engage with their target audience. In today's digital age, social media marketing has become a crucial component of any brand's marketing strategy. Here are several reasons why social media marketing is of utmost importance for brands:

- **Widespread Reach:** Social media platforms have an enormous user base, making them an ideal channel for brands to reach a vast and diverse audience. With just a few clicks, businesses can connect with potential customers from all corners of the world. This level of reach is unparalleled compared to traditional marketing methods.

- **Enhanced Brand Awareness:** Social media platforms offer brands an opportunity to showcase their products, services, and values to a global audience. By consistently sharing engaging and relevant content, brands can raise awareness and create a strong brand presence. As users engage with the content, it gets shared, further increasing brand visibility and recognition.

- **Targeted Advertising:** Social media platforms provide robust targeting options that allow brands to tailor their marketing efforts to specific demographics, interests, and behaviors. By utilizing the wealth of data available on these platforms, businesses can ensure that their ads are shown to the most relevant audience, maximizing the chances of conversion and return on investment.

- **Increased Customer Engagement**: Social media is a two-way communication channel, enabling brands to directly engage with their customers. Through comments, messages, and reviews, brands can build meaningful relationships and foster a sense of loyalty and trust. Engaging with customers also provides valuable insights into their preferences, enabling businesses to refine their products or services based on customer feedback.

- **Cost-Effective Marketing:** Social media marketing is generally more cost-effective compared to traditional marketing channels. Setting up social media profiles and running targeted ads require a fraction of the investment needed for television, print, or radio advertising. This makes social media marketing an attractive option, particularly for small and medium-sized businesses with limited budgets.

- **Influencer Partnerships:** Social media influencers have gained significant prominence, and partnering with them can greatly amplify a brand's reach and credibility. Influencers have loyal followers who trust their recommendations, making them powerful brand advocates. Collaborating with influencers allows brands to tap into their audience, effectively leveraging their influence to promote products or services.

- **Real-Time Feedback and Analysis:** Social media platforms offer extensive analytics and reporting tools, providing brands with real-time feedback on the performance of their campaigns. Brands can monitor engagement metrics, track conversions, and measure the effectiveness of their social media marketing efforts.

This data-driven approach allows businesses to make informed decisions, refine their strategies, and optimize their marketing campaigns for better results.

In conclusion, social media marketing has revolutionized the way brands interact with their audience. Its importance lies in its ability to connect businesses with a vast global audience, raise brand awareness, facilitate targeted advertising, foster customer engagement, and provide cost-effective marketing solutions. Brands that effectively leverage social media platforms can gain a competitive edge, enhance their brand equity, and drive business growth in the digital era.

1.3 Trends and Opportunities in Social Media Marketing

Social media marketing continues to be a rapidly evolving field with new trends and opportunities emerging regularly.

Here are some key trends and opportunities in social media marketing:

- **Video Content Dominance:** Video content has become increasingly popular and is dominating social media platforms. Short-form videos, live videos, and stories are highly engaging and offer brands an opportunity to connect with their audience in an authentic and dynamic way. Platforms like **TikTok, Instagram Reels, and YouTube** continue to gain momentum, and brands should leverage these platforms to create compelling video content.

- **Influencer Marketing:** Influencer marketing has proven to be an effective strategy for brands to reach their target audience. Collaborating with influencers who have a significant following and influence in a particular niche can help increase brand awareness, credibility, and engagement. Micro-influencers (those with smaller but highly engaged audiences) are also gaining traction as they offer more affordable partnerships and niche expertise.

- **Social Commerce:** Social media platforms are increasingly integrating e-commerce features, making it easier for brands to sell products directly to their audience. Features like shoppable posts, product tags, and in-app checkouts enable seamless shopping experiences. Brands should optimize their social media presence to drive conversions and leverage platforms like **Instagram Shopping, Facebook Marketplace, and Pinterest Shop**.

- **Personalized and Authentic Content:** Consumers are seeking personalized and authentic experiences on social media. Brands that can deliver tailored content and communicate their values in an authentic way are more likely to resonate with their audience. User-generated content (UGC), behind-the-scenes glimpses, and transparent storytelling can help create a sense of authenticity and build trust.

- **Augmented Reality (AR) and Virtual Reality (VR):** AR and VR technologies are expanding the possibilities of social media marketing. Brands can use AR filters and effects to enhance user experiences, offer virtual try-on experiences, or create immersive branded content. Platforms like Snapchat, Instagram, and Facebook are providing tools for brands to leverage AR and VR for engaging marketing campaigns.

- **Social Listening and Customer Engagement:** Social media platforms provide valuable insights into consumer preferences and conversations. Brands can leverage social listening tools to monitor mentions, sentiment, and trends related to their industry. This allows them to understand their audience better and engage in meaningful conversations. Prompt and authentic responses to customer queries and feedback can enhance brand reputation and loyalty.

- **Data-driven Decision Making:** Social media platforms offer robust analytics and data tracking capabilities. Brands should leverage these insights to measure the effectiveness of their campaigns, identify trends, and make data-driven decisions. Understanding key metrics such as reach, engagement, conversion rates, and audience demographics can help optimize marketing strategies for better results.

- **Privacy and Data Protection:** With increasing concerns around privacy and data protection, brands need to be transparent and compliant with regulations. Users are becoming more aware of their privacy rights, and brands that prioritize data security and ethical practices can build trust with their audience.

- **Niche and Emerging Platforms:** While major platforms like Facebook, Instagram, and Twitter continue to dominate, niche and emerging platforms are gaining popularity. For example, TikTok has seen explosive growth and is attracting a diverse user base. Brands should explore these platforms to reach specific audiences and leverage their unique features and trends.

- **Artificial Intelligence (AI) and Automation:** AI-powered tools and automation are transforming social media marketing. Chatbots, automated scheduling, sentiment analysis, and content curation tools can streamline processes, improve efficiency, and enhance the overall customer experience.

It's important for brands to stay agile, keep up with the latest trends, and adapt their social media marketing strategies to capitalize on emerging opportunities.

PART I

Building a Strong Foundation

2. Defining your brand identity

Defining your brand identity is crucial for establishing a strong and memorable presence in the marketplace. It encompasses the essence of your brand, including its values, personality, and visual elements. Your brand identity is what distinguishes you from competitors and shapes how your target audience perceives and connects with your business. Here are some key components to consider when defining your brand identity:

- **Purpose and Values:** Start by clarifying your brand's purpose— the reason your business exists beyond making a profit. What core values drive your company? Your purpose and values should align with your target audience's beliefs and resonate with them on a deeper level.

- **Target Audience:** Understand your target audience's demographics, preferences, and aspirations. Tailor your brand identity to appeal to their specific needs and desires. Consider their age, location, interests, and psychographic factors to create a brand that speaks directly to them.

- **Brand Personality:** Define your brand's personality traits as if it were a person. Is your brand playful and energetic, or serious and authoritative? Think about how you want your audience to feel when interacting with your brand and develop a personality that reflects those emotions.

- **Unique Selling Proposition (USP):** Determine your USP—the unique value or benefit that sets you apart from competitors. Highlight what makes your brand special and communicate it consistently across all brand touchpoints.

- **Visual Identity:** Your visual identity includes your logo, color palette, typography, and overall design style. These elements should be carefully chosen to reflect your brand's personality and resonate with your target audience. Consistency in visual branding is crucial to build recognition and create a cohesive brand experience.

- **Tone of Voice:** Establish a consistent tone of voice that aligns with your brand personality. Consider the language, vocabulary, and style of communication that will engage your audience effectively. Whether it's conversational, formal, or humorous, ensure your tone is consistent across all channels and interactions.

- **Brand Storytelling:** Craft a compelling brand narrative that communicates your values, mission, and unique journey. Use storytelling techniques to engage your audience emotionally and forge a deeper connection. Showcasing the human side of your brand can help foster trust and loyalty.

- **Brand Guidelines:** Consolidate all the elements of your brand identity into comprehensive guidelines. These guidelines serve as a reference for maintaining consistency in messaging, design, and communication across different platforms and channels.

Remember, building a strong brand identity is an ongoing process. It requires constant monitoring, adaptation, and reinforcement to stay relevant and resonate with your evolving audience. Stay true to your core values while embracing innovation and market trends to keep your brand identity fresh and engaging.

2.1 Branding Basics

Branding is an essential aspect of any business or organization. It encompasses the perception, values, and personality associated with a product, service, or company. A strong brand identity can differentiate you from competitors, build trust with customers, and foster loyalty. To help you establish a solid foundation for your brand, here are some key branding basics to consider:

- **Define Your Brand:** Start by clearly defining your brand's purpose, mission, and values. Determine what sets your brand apart and what you want to be known for. This will shape your brand's personality and guide all aspects of your branding efforts.

Know Your Target Audience: Understanding your target audience is crucial for effective branding. Identify their needs, preferences, and pain points. This knowledge will help you tailor your brand messaging and visuals to resonate with your audience and create a genuine connection.

- **Craft Your Brand Identity:** Your brand identity encompasses visual elements such as logo, color palette, typography, and imagery. These elements should be carefully chosen to reflect your brand's personality and resonate with your target audience. Consistency is key - ensure that your brand identity is applied consistently across all touchpoints.

- **Develop Your Brand Voice:** Your brand voice is the tone and style of your brand's communication. It should align with your brand's personality and appeal to your target audience. Whether your voice is formal, casual, humorous, or authoritative, maintaining consistency in your brand voice will help create a recognizable and cohesive brand experience.

- **Build Brand Guidelines:** Brand guidelines serve as a blueprint for how your brand should be represented. They outline rules and specifications for logo usage, color codes, typography, tone of voice, and more. Brand guidelines help maintain consistency across various platforms and ensure that your brand's visual and verbal communication is coherent.

- **Create Compelling Brand Messaging:** Your brand messaging should clearly communicate your brand's value proposition, key benefits, and unique selling points. Craft concise and compelling taglines, slogans, and brand stories that resonate with your target audience. Your messaging should evoke emotions, connect with your audience's aspirations, and differentiate your brand from competitors.

- **Deliver Consistent Brand Experience:** Consistency is crucial for building a strong brand. Ensure that your brand's visual identity, messaging, and customer experience are consistent across all touchpoints, including your website, social media profiles, packaging, advertising, and customer interactions. Consistency builds trust and reinforces your brand's identity.

- **Foster Brand Advocacy:** Encourage your customers to become brand advocates by providing exceptional experiences, products, or services. Positive word-of-mouth recommendations from satisfied customers can significantly impact your brand's reputation and growth. Engage with your audience on social media, encourage user-generated content, and cultivate a community around your brand.

- **Adapt and Evolve:** Brands need to evolve and adapt to stay relevant. Monitor market trends, customer feedback, and industry changes. Continuously refine and improve your brand strategy, visual identity, messaging, and customer experience to remain competitive and meet evolving customer expectations.

Remember, branding is not just about logos and slogans; it's about creating a meaningful and memorable experience for your audience. By following these branding basics and consistently delivering on your brand promise, you can establish a strong brand identity that resonates with your target audience and drives long-term success.

2.2 Identifying your target audience

Identifying your target audience is a crucial step in developing an effective marketing strategy and ensuring the success of your business or project. By understanding who your target audience is, you can tailor your messaging, products, and services to meet their specific needs and preferences. Here are some key steps to help you identify your target audience:

- **Define your product or service:** Start by clearly defining what you are offering. Understand its features, benefits, and unique selling points. This will help you identify the characteristics and qualities that make your offering valuable to potential customers.

- **Conduct market research:** Perform thorough market research to gather information about your industry, competitors, and potential customers. Utilize both qualitative and quantitative research methods to gain insights into consumer behavior, demographics, psychographics, and purchasing patterns.

- **Analyze exlsting customer data:** If you already have an existing customer base, analyze their data to identify common characteristics and patterns. Look for demographic information such as age, gender, location, income level, and occupation. Additionally, examine their interests, preferences, and purchasing behavior to gain a deeper understanding of their motivations.

- **Create buyer personas:** Based on the data collected, create detailed buyer personas that represent your ideal customers. A buyer persona is a fictional profile that encompasses the characteristics, needs, and goals of a specific segment of your target audience. Give each persona a name, demographics, and psychographics to humanize them and facilitate better decision-making.

- **Identify pain points and motivations:** Explore the pain points, challenges, and aspirations of your target audience. Understand what problems they are trying to solve and how your product or service can provide a solution. This understanding will help you create compelling messaging that resonates with their needs and desires.

- **Evaluate competition:** Study your competitors and analyze their target audience. Identify the gaps and opportunities that exist within the market and assess how your offering can differentiate itself to attract a specific segment of customers.

- **Test and iterate:** Once you have identified your target audience, test your marketing messages, channels, and strategies to see how well they resonate. Monitor the response and feedback from your audience, and be willing to make adjustments and iterate based on the results.

Remember, identifying your target audience is an ongoing process. As your business grows and evolves, so may your target audience. Stay attuned to market trends, customer feedback, and changes in consumer behavior to ensure that your target audience remains accurately defined.

2.3 Crafting Your Unique Value Proposition

Your unique value proposition (UVP) is a concise statement that communicates the unique benefits and value your product, service, or brand offers to your target audience. It is a crucial element in differentiating yourself from competitors and capturing the attention of your potential customers. Crafting an effective UVP requires careful thought and consideration. Here are some steps to help you create a compelling and unique value proposition:

- **Identify your target audience:** Before you can create a UVP, you need to have a clear understanding of who your target audience is. Define their demographics, needs, desires, and pain points. The more specific and detailed your understanding of your audience, the better you can tailor your value proposition to resonate with them.

- **Define your unique selling points:** What sets your product, service, or brand apart from others in the market? Identify the unique features, benefits, or qualities that differentiate you. These can include aspects such as superior quality, innovative technology, exceptional customer service, or a specific niche focus. Consider both functional and emotional aspects that appeal to your target audience.

- **Focus on solving a problem or fulfilling a need:** A strong value proposition addresses a specific problem or need that your target audience has. It should clearly communicate how your product or service solves their problem or fulfills their need better than anyone else. By highlighting the benefits and outcomes, you can demonstrate the value you offer.

- **Keep it concise and clear:** Your UVP should be concise and easy to understand. Avoid using jargon or complex language that might confuse your audience. Aim for a statement that can be easily communicated and remembered. Ideally, your UVP should be a single sentence or a brief paragraph.

- **Communicate the value, not just features:** While it's essential to highlight your unique features, your UVP should primarily focus on the value and benefits you bring to your customers. Think about the ultimate result or transformation your target audience will experience by choosing your product or service. This helps create an emotional connection and emphasizes the impact you can make in their lives.

- **Test and iterate:** Crafting an effective UVP often requires testing and refining. Share your UVP with colleagues, partners, or even potential customers to gather feedback. Test different variations and analyze the responses to see which resonates the most with your audience. Iterate and refine until you have a value proposition that consistently grabs attention and generates interest.

- **Align with your brand:** Your UVP should align with your brand's identity, values, and positioning. It should be consistent with the overall messaging and image you want to portray. This ensures a cohesive and memorable brand experience for your customers.

Remember, your UVP is not set in stone. As your business evolves and market conditions change, you may need to revisit and update your value proposition. Continuously monitor your audience's needs and expectations to stay relevant and maintain a competitive edge.

Crafting a compelling and unique value proposition is a critical step in attracting and retaining customers. By clearly communicating the value you offer and how it meets the needs of your target audience, you can differentiate yourself from competitors and establish a strong position in the market.

Setting SMART Goals for Social Media Marketing

3.1 Understanding SMART Goals

Setting SMART goals for social media marketing is essential for ensuring that your efforts are focused, measurable, and ultimately effective. SMART is an acronym that stands for Specific, Measurable, Achievable, Relevant, and Time-bound. By following these principles, you can create goals that are well-defined and actionable, leading to better results in your social media marketing campaigns. Here's a breakdown of how to apply the SMART framework to your social media goals:

- **Specific:** Your goals should be clear and well-defined. Instead of a vague goal like "increase social media presence," specify what you want to achieve. For example, "Increase Instagram followers by 20% in three months" or "Generate 100 leads per month through Facebook advertising."

- **Measurable:** It's crucial to set goals that can be measured quantitatively. This allows you to track progress and determine whether you've achieved your objectives. Define metrics such as the number of followers, engagement rate, click-through rate, conversions, or revenue generated through social media campaigns.

- **Achievable:** While it's important to set ambitious goals, they should also be realistic and attainable.

Consider your available resources, budget, and capabilities. Setting a goal to gain a million followers in a week when you have a small following and limited resources may not be achievable. Make sure your goals stretch your capabilities but are still within reach.

- **Relevant:** Ensure that your social media goals align with your overall marketing objectives and the broader business goals. They should contribute to your organization's growth and be relevant to your target audience. For example, if your company aims to increase brand awareness, a relevant goal could be to boost social media reach and engagement.

- **Time-bound:** Set a specific timeline for achieving your goals. This adds a sense of urgency and helps you stay accountable. Determine if your goals are short-term (e.g., one month) or long-term (e.g., six months) and establish milestones along the way. Having a deadline will motivate you to take action and evaluate your progress regularly.

Example of a SMART goal for social media marketing:

"Increase website traffic from social media platforms by 30% in the next three months by posting engaging content, running targeted ad campaigns, and optimizing landing pages for conversions."

Remember that setting SMART goals is just the beginning. Regularly monitor your progress, make adjustments if necessary, and analyze the results to refine your social media marketing strategy. By using SMART goals, you can ensure that your efforts are focused, measurable, and aligned with your overall marketing objectives.

3.2 Aligning Goals with Business Objectives

Goal alignment is the process of ensuring that all employees are working towards the same goals. This is essential for any organization that wants to be successful. When goals are aligned, everyone is pulling in the same direction, and there is a greater chance of achieving success.

There are a number of benefits to goal alignment, including:

Increased productivity: When employees know what they are working towards, they are more likely to be productive.

Improved morale: Employees who feel like they are part of something bigger are more likely to be motivated and engaged.

Reduced costs: When goals are aligned, there is less duplication of effort and resources.

Enhanced decision-making: When everyone is working towards the same goals, it is easier to make decisions that are in the best interests of the organization.

There are a number of things that organizations can do to align their goals, including:

Set clear goals: The first step is to set clear and measurable goals. This will help to ensure that everyone knows what they are working towards.

Communicate goals: Once goals have been set, they need to be communicated to all employees. This can be done through meetings, newsletters, or other communication channels.

Track progress: It is important to track progress towards goals so that adjustments can be made as needed. This can be done through regular check-ins, performance reviews, or other methods.

Celebrate successes: It is important to celebrate successes along the way. This will help to keep employees motivated and engaged.

Goal alignment is an essential part of any successful organization. By following the steps above, organizations can ensure that everyone is working towards the same goals and that they are more likely to achieve success.

Here are some additional tips for aligning goals with business objectives:

Make sure that goals are SMART: Specific, measurable, achievable, relevant, and time-bound.

Involve employees in the goal-setting process. This will help to ensure that they are committed to achieving the goals.

Regularly review goals and make adjustments as needed. This will help to ensure that goals are still relevant and achievable.

Provide feedback and support to employees. This will help them to stay on track and achieve their goals.

By following these tips, organizations can create a culture of goal alignment and achieve their business objectives.

3.3 Key Performance Indicators (KPIs) for Social Media Marketing

Key Performance Indicators (KPIs) are the metrics used to measure the success of a social media marketing campaign. They can be used to track a variety of factors, such as reach, engagement, website traffic, and sales.

The best KPIs for your business will vary depending on your specific goals and objectives. However, some common KPIs that businesses use to measure their social media performance include:

- **Reach:** This is the number of people who have seen your content.

- **Engagement:** This is the number of people who have interacted with your content, such as by liking, sharing, or commenting.

- **Website traffic:** This is the number of people who have visited your website after clicking on a link from your social media channels.

- **Sales:** This is the number of products or services you have sold as a result of your social media marketing efforts.

In addition to these common KPIs, there are a number of other metrics that you may want to track, depending on your specific goals. For example, if you are trying to increase brand awareness, you may want to track the number of times your brand is mentioned on social media. Or, if you are trying to generate leads, you may want to track the number of people who sign up for your email list after clicking on a link from your social media channels.

It is important to track a variety of KPIs so that you can get a complete picture of your social media performance. By tracking these metrics, you can identify what is working and what is not, and make adjustments to your strategy accordingly.

Here are some tips for choosing the right KPIs for your business:

Start by setting clear goals. What do you want to achieve with your social media marketing efforts? Once you know your goals, you can choose KPIs that will help you measure your progress.

Consider your target audience. Who are you trying to reach with your social media marketing? Choose KPIs that will help you track how well you are reaching your target audience.

Choose KPIs that are relevant to your business. Not all KPIs are created equal. Choose KPIs that are relevant to your business goals and objectives.

Track your KPIs over time. The best way to see how your social media marketing is performing is to track your KPIs over time. This will help you identify trends and make adjustments to your strategy as needed.

Tracking your KPIs is an essential part of any social media marketing strategy. By tracking your KPIs, you can ensure that your social media marketing efforts are working and that you are achieving your goals.

Developing a Content Strategy

4.1 Content Marketing Fundamentals

Content marketing is a strategic approach to marketing that involves creating and distributing valuable, relevant, and consistent content to attract and engage a target audience. It focuses on providing useful information, solving problems, and building relationships with potential customers, ultimately driving profitable customer action.

Here are some fundamental principles and components of content marketing:

- **Audience Understanding:** Before creating content, it's crucial to understand your target audience's needs, interests, and pain points. Conduct market research, analyze customer data, and develop buyer personas to gain insights into their preferences and behaviors.

- **Clear Objectives:** Define your content marketing goals. Common objectives include increasing brand awareness, generating leads, boosting website traffic, enhancing customer engagement, or establishing thought leadership. Setting clear objectives helps you measure success and align your content strategy accordingly.

- **Content Strategy:** Develop a comprehensive content strategy that outlines your goals, target audience, key messages, content formats, distribution channels, and a content calendar. Consider the different stages of the customer journey and create content that resonates with your audience at each stage.

- **Quality Content Creation:** Create high-quality, valuable content that addresses your audience's needs and interests. Focus on delivering relevant information, solving problems, and offering unique insights. Use different content formats such as blog posts, videos, infographics, ebooks, podcasts, and social media posts to cater to diverse audience preferences.

- **Consistency and Frequency:** Consistency is crucial in content marketing. Develop a consistent brand voice, style, and tone across your content. Regularly publish new content to keep your audience engaged and build anticipation. However, prioritize quality over quantity to ensure your content maintains its value.

- **SEO Optimization:** Optimize your content for search engines to improve its visibility and reach. Conduct keyword research to identify relevant search terms and incorporate them naturally into your content. Focus on on-page SEO elements such as meta tags, headings, and URL structure. Additionally, build backlinks and promote your content to improve its ranking.

- **Distribution and Promotion:** Develop a distribution strategy to reach your target audience effectively. Leverage various channels such as your website, blog, social media platforms, email newsletters, guest posting, and influencer partnerships. Actively promote your content through social sharing, paid advertising, email campaigns, and other promotional tactics.

- **Engagement and Interaction:** Encourage audience engagement by facilitating comments, discussions, and social sharing. Respond to comments and inquiries promptly to build a relationship with your audience. Encourage user-generated content and incorporate it into your strategy. Monitor and analyze engagement metrics to understand what resonates with your audience.

- **Measurement and Analysis:** Track and measure the performance of your content marketing efforts. Use analytics tools to monitor key metrics such as website traffic, engagement, conversion rates, and social media metrics. Analyze the data to identify successful content pieces and optimize your strategy based on insights.

- **Iteration and Improvement:** Content marketing is an iterative process. Continuously evaluate your content strategy, experiment with different approaches, and learn from your successes and failures. Stay updated with industry trends and adapt your strategy accordingly to ensure ongoing success.

Remember that content marketing is a long-term strategy that requires patience and consistency. By consistently providing value to your target audience, you can build trust, credibility, and brand loyalty, ultimately driving business growth.

4.2 Creating Engaging and Shareable Content

In today's digital age, content is king. With so much information available at our fingertips, it's more important than ever to create content that is engaging and shareable.

There are a few key things you can do to create content that people will want to read, watch, and share.

Know your audience. Who are you writing for? What do they care about? What kind of content will they find interesting and valuable?

Create content that is relevant to your audience. Don't just write about anything and everything. Focus on topics that are of interest to your target audience.

Make your content visually appealing. People are more likely to engage with content that is visually appealing. Use high-quality images and videos to break up your text and make your content more visually appealing.

Write in a clear and concise style. People are busy and they don't have time to read through long, rambling articles. Get to the point quickly and clearly.

Use strong headlines and calls to action. Your headline is the first thing people will see, so make sure it's attention-grabbing. A strong call to action will encourage people to take the next step, whether it's reading your article, watching your video, or signing up for your email list.

Promote your content. Once you've created great content, don't just sit back and wait for people to find it. Share it on social media, email it to your subscribers, and submit it to relevant websites and publications.

By following these tips, you can create content that is engaging and shareable. This will help you reach a wider audience, build relationships with your target audience, and grow your business.

Here are some additional tips for creating shareable content:

Use humor. People love to laugh, so using humor in your content is a great way to get people's attention.

Be controversial. People love to debate, so if you can create content that is controversial, you're more likely to get people talking.

Be timely. People are more likely to share content that is timely and relevant to current events.

Use visuals. People are more likely to engage with content that includes visuals, such as images, videos, and infographics.

Make it easy to share. Make sure your content is easy to share on social media and other platforms. Include social sharing buttons on your website and blog posts, and make sure your content is optimized for search engines.

By following these tips, you can create content that is engaging and shareable. This will help you reach a wider audience, build relationships with your target audience, and grow your business.

4.3 Tailoring Content for Different Social Media Platforms

Social media platforms are a great way to connect with your audience and share your content with the world. But with so many different platforms to choose from, it can be tough to know where to start. That's why it's important to tailor your content for each platform.

Here are a few tips for tailoring your content for different social media platforms:

- **Facebook:** Facebook is a great platform for sharing news, updates, and behind-the-scenes content. Your posts should be informative and engaging, and they should be relevant to your audience.

- **Twitter:** Twitter is a great platform for sharing short, concise messages. Your tweets should be to the point and they should be something that will make people stop and take notice.

- **Instagram:** Instagram is a visual platform, so your posts should be visually appealing. Use high-quality images and videos, and make sure your captions are interesting and engaging.

- **Pinterest:** Pinterest is a great platform for sharing inspiration. Your pins should be visually appealing and they should be something that will make people want to learn more.

- **LinkedIn:** LinkedIn is a professional platform, so your posts should be professional and informative. Your posts should be relevant to your industry and they should be something that will add value to your audience.

By tailoring your content for each platform, you'll be more likely to reach your target audience and engage with them.

Here are some additional tips for tailoring your content for different social media platforms:

- **Use different types of content:** Don't just post text. Mix it up with images, videos, infographics, and other types of content.

- **Use relevant hashtags:** Hashtags are a great way to get your content seen by more people. Use hashtags that are relevant to your industry and your target audience.

- **Engage with your audience:** Respond to comments and questions, and participate in conversations. The more you engage with your audience, the more likely they are to engage with your content.

- **Track your results:** Use analytics to track how your content is performing. This will help you see what's working and what's not, so you can adjust your strategy accordingly.

By following these tips, you can tailor your content for different social media platforms and reach your target audience with your message.

Part II

Mastering Social Media Platforms

5. Leveraging Facebook for Brand Awareness

Facebook is a powerful platform for businesses of all sizes to reach new customers and build brand awareness. With over 2.9 billion active users, Facebook offers a vast audience for businesses to target.

There are a number of ways to leverage Facebook for brand awareness. Here are a few tips:

Create engaging content. The key to success on Facebook is creating content that people will want to engage with. This could include anything from funny videos to informative articles. The more people who engage with your content, the more likely they are to remember your brand.

Use Facebook ads. Facebook ads can be a great way to reach a wider audience and target your ads to specific demographics. You can use ads to promote your website, products, or services.

Run contests and giveaways. Contests and giveaways are a great way to generate excitement around your brand and attract new followers. When people enter a contest, they're more likely to learn about your brand and what you have to offer.

Partner with influencers. Influencers are people who have a large following on social media. Partnering with an influencer can help you reach a new audience and get your brand in front of more people.

By following these tips, you can leverage Facebook to build brand awareness and reach new customers.

Here are some additional tips for leveraging Facebook for brand awareness:

Use high-quality images and videos. Visual content is more likely to be engaging than text-only content. When creating images and videos for Facebook, make sure they are high-quality and relevant to your brand.

Use a strong call to action. Tell people what you want them to do after they see your content. Do you want them to visit your website? Sign up for your email list? Make sure your call to action is clear and concise.

Track your results. It's important to track the results of your Facebook campaigns so you can see what's working and what's not. Use Facebook

Insights to track metrics like reach, engagement, and website traffic.

By following these tips, you can leverage Facebook to build brand awareness and reach new customers.

5.1 Creating a Compelling Facebook Page

A compelling Facebook Page is one that is well-designed, informative, and engaging. It should be easy to find and navigate, and it should provide value to its users. Here are some tips for creating a compelling Facebook Page:

Choose a clear and concise name. Your Facebook Page name should be easy to remember and relevant to your business. It should also be unique, so that it's easy for people to find you.

Add a professional profile picture and cover photo. Your profile picture and cover photo should be high-quality and visually appealing. They should also be relevant to your business and accurately represent your brand.

Complete your About section. Your About section should provide users with more information about your business, such as your mission statement, contact information, and hours of operation.

Post interesting and engaging content. The key to a successful Facebook Page is to post content that your audience will find interesting and engaging. This could include blog posts, articles, videos, images, or even just status updates.

Promote your Page. Once you've created a compelling Facebook Page, you need to promote it so that people can find it. You can do this by sharing your Page on other social media platforms, adding it to your website, or running paid advertising campaigns.

By following these tips, you can create a compelling Facebook Page that will help you connect with your audience and grow your business.

Here are some additional tips for creating a compelling Facebook Page:

Use visuals. People are more likely to engage with content that includes visuals, such as images, videos, and infographics.

Be consistent. Post new content on a regular basis so that your audience has something to come back for.

Be interactive. Encourage your audience to comment, like, and share your content.

Respond to comments and questions. This shows that you're engaged with your audience and that you care about their feedback.

Use Facebook's analytics tools to track your progress. This will help you see what's working and what's not, so that you can make changes to improve your Page.

By following these tips, you can create a compelling Facebook Page that will help you connect with your audience and grow your business.

5.2 Optimizing Facebook Posts for Maximum Engagement

Optimizing Facebook posts for maximum engagement is crucial for businesses and individuals alike who want to reach a wider audience and increase their social media presence. Here are some strategies and tips to help you optimize your Facebook posts and boost engagement:

- **Know your audience**: Understanding your target audience is essential for creating content that resonates with them.

Research their demographics, interests, and preferences to tailor your posts accordingly. Use Facebook Insights or other analytics tools to gain insights into your audience's behavior and engagement patterns.

- **Eye-catching visuals:** Visual content is highly effective in capturing attention and increasing engagement on Facebook. Use high-quality images, videos, and graphics that are relevant to your post and visually appealing. Incorporate your branding elements to maintain consistency and make your content easily recognizable.

- **Compelling headlines:** Your post's headline or caption is the first thing users see, so it needs to be attention-grabbing. Craft concise and compelling headlines that pique curiosity, evoke emotion, or offer value to your audience. Consider using action words, asking questions, or using numbers to make your posts stand out.

- **Use hashtags strategically:** Hashtags can help expand your reach beyond your immediate followers. Research relevant and popular hashtags related to your content and industry. Limit the number of hashtags to a few well-chosen ones that are directly related to your post, rather than using too many unrelated ones.

- **Engage with your audience:** Actively engage with your audience by responding to comments, messages, and feedback. Promptly address questions, provide additional information, and encourage discussions. This interaction builds a sense of community and encourages others to engage with your content as well.

- **Timing is key:** Pay attention to the timing of your posts. Experiment with different posting times and track the engagement metrics to determine the optimal posting schedule for your audience. Consider posting when your target audience is most likely to be active on Facebook, such as during lunch breaks, evenings, or weekends.

- **Utilize Facebook features:** Facebook offers various features to enhance engagement. Experiment with live videos, polls, stories, and interactive content formats to increase user participation and drive engagement. These features often receive higher visibility and encourage users to spend more time interacting with your posts.

- **Analyze and refine:** Regularly review the performance of your Facebook posts using Facebook Insights or other analytics tools. Analyze engagement metrics such as reach, likes, comments, and shares to identify patterns and understand what type of content resonates best with your audience. Use this information to refine your content strategy and optimize future posts.

Remember, consistent optimization and experimentation are key to finding the most effective strategies for your specific audience. Keep testing different approaches, analyzing the results, and adapting your content accordingly. By following these tips, you can maximize engagement on your Facebook posts and build a thriving online community.

5.3 Facebook Advertising Strategies

Facebook has emerged as one of the most influential platforms for digital advertising, offering businesses a vast audience and robust targeting options. To leverage the full potential of Facebook advertising, it's crucial to develop effective strategies that align with your marketing goals and reach your target audience. Here are some key strategies to consider:

- **Define Your Objectives:** Start by clearly outlining your advertising objectives. Are you aiming to increase brand awareness, drive website traffic, generate leads, or boost sales? Defining your goals will shape your entire advertising strategy and help you measure success.

- **Audience Targeting:** Facebook provides powerful targeting options based on demographics, interests, behaviors, and more. Utilize this feature to narrow down your audience and ensure your ads reach the right people. Define your target audience based on factors such as age, location, interests, and purchasing behaviors.

- **Compelling Ad Creatives:** Capture your audience's attention with visually appealing and engaging ad creatives. Use high-quality images or videos that convey your brand message effectively. Craft compelling ad copy that is concise, persuasive, and encourages action. Test different variations to identify the most effective combination.

- **Ad Formats:** Facebook offers a variety of ad formats, including image ads, video ads, carousel ads, and canvas ads. Experiment with different formats to see what resonates best with your audience and aligns with your campaign goals. Video ads, in particular, tend to have higher engagement rates.

- **Custom Audiences and Lookalike Audiences**: Leverage Facebook's custom audience feature to target specific segments of your existing customer base. You can create custom audiences based on factors like email lists, website visitors, or app users. Additionally, use lookalike audiences to reach new users who share similar characteristics with your existing customers.

- **Retargeting:** Implement a retargeting strategy to re-engage users who have previously interacted with your brand. Set up Facebook Pixel on your website to track user behavior and create custom audiences for retargeting. Tailor your ads to remind users of their previous interactions and offer incentives to encourage conversions.

- **A/B Testing:** Constantly test and refine your ads to optimize their performance. Conduct A/B tests with different ad elements such as headlines, images, calls-to-action, or targeting options. Analyze the results and make data-driven decisions to improve the effectiveness of your campaigns.

- **Ad Placement:** Facebook offers various ad placements, including the news feed, right column, instant articles, and stories. Experiment with different placements to find the ones that generate the best results for your specific campaign. Remember to optimize your ads for mobile devices, as a significant portion of Facebook users access the platform through mobile devices.

- **Budgeting and Optimization:** Set a realistic budget for your Facebook advertising campaigns. Monitor your campaigns regularly and make adjustments to optimize performance. Facebook's ad manager provides detailed analytics and performance metrics that can help you identify areas for improvement and allocate your budget effectively.

- **Ongoing Analysis and Iteration:** Continuously analyze the performance of your Facebook ad campaigns. Monitor key metrics such as click-through rates, conversions, cost per acquisition, and return on ad spend. Based on the insights gained, make necessary adjustments to your targeting, creative elements, or bidding strategies.

Remember that Facebook advertising requires ongoing monitoring and optimization. Stay updated with the latest features and changes in Facebook's advertising platform to ensure your strategies remain effective. By implementing these strategies and adapting them to your unique business needs, you can maximize the impact of your Facebook advertising campaigns and achieve your marketing objectives.

Maximizing Instagram for Visual Storytelling

6.1 Instagram Profile Optimization

Your Instagram profile serves as your virtual business card, making a strong first impression on potential followers and customers. Optimizing your profile is essential for attracting the right audience and maximizing engagement.

By following a few key strategies, you can enhance your Instagram profile and make it stand out from the crowd. Here are some tips for effective Instagram profile optimization:

- **Choose a compelling username:** Your username should be memorable, relevant to your brand or personal identity, and easy to spell. Avoid using complex or ambiguous usernames that may confuse potential followers.

- **Craft a captivating bio:** Your bio is a valuable space to introduce yourself or your brand, convey your unique selling proposition, and showcase your personality. Keep it concise, engaging, and use relevant keywords to improve discoverability.

- **Utilize keywords strategically:** Including relevant keywords in your bio, captions, and hashtags can improve your profile's visibility in Instagram searches. Research popular keywords in your niche and incorporate them naturally into your content.

- **Select an appealing profile picture:** Your profile picture is a visual representation of your brand or personal identity. Choose a high-quality image that is easily recognizable and reflects the essence of your account.

- **Add a link in your bio:** Instagram allows you to include a clickable link in your bio. Utilize this feature to direct users to your website, blog, or other important destinations. Consider using link shortening services to make the link more visually appealing and trackable.

- **Highlight your best content with featured stories**: Instagram's "Highlights" feature allows you to save and display your best-performing stories permanently on your profile. Use this to showcase your top products, services, or any other important information.

- **Use relevant hashtags**: Including hashtags in your captions helps categorize your content and increase its discoverability. Research popular and niche-specific hashtags to reach your target audience effectively.

- **Engage with your audience:** Actively respond to comments, direct messages, and mentions to foster a sense of community and build strong relationships with your followers. Show genuine interest and appreciation for their support.

- **Post consistently:** Regularly sharing high-quality, relevant content keeps your profile active and attracts new followers. Create a content calendar and stick to a consistent posting schedule to maintain engagement and visibility.

- **Monitor and analyze your profile's performance:** Take advantage of Instagram's analytics tools to gain insights into your audience demographics, post reach, and engagement. Use this data to refine your content strategy and optimize your profile further.

Remember, Instagram profile optimization is an ongoing process. Continuously monitor your profile's performance, stay updated with new features and trends, and adapt your strategy accordingly. By implementing these tips, you can effectively optimize your Instagram profile and increase your chances of success on the platform.

6.2 Creating Captivating Visual Content

In today's visually-driven world, capturing the attention of your audience has become more challenging than ever before. With the constant influx of information and images, it's crucial to create captivating visual content that stands out and engages viewers. Whether you're a marketer, designer, or content creator, mastering the art of visual storytelling can make a significant impact on your success. Here are some key principles and strategies to help you create captivating visual content that captivates and resonates with your audience.

- **Know Your Audience**: Before diving into the creation process, it's essential to understand who your target audience is. Research their preferences, demographics, and interests. By gaining insights into their needs and desires, you can tailor your visual content to effectively connect with them on a deeper level.

- **Develop a Clear Message**: Every visual piece should convey a clear and concise message. Determine the purpose and objective of your content before you begin designing. Whether it's promoting a product, sharing information, or evoking emotion, your visuals should align with your intended message.

- **Use High-Quality Imagery**: The quality of your visuals plays a significant role in capturing attention. Invest in high-resolution images and videos that are visually appealing and reflect your brand's aesthetic. Avoid pixelation or blurry visuals, as they can diminish the impact of your content.

- **Leverage Color Psychology**: Colors have a powerful influence on human emotions and perceptions. Utilize color psychology to evoke specific feelings or associations in your audience. Understand the meaning behind different colors and select a palette that aligns with your message and brand identity. Consistency in color usage can also help in creating a cohesive visual experience.

- **Focus on Visual Hierarchy**: Effective visual content follows a hierarchy that guides the viewer's attention. Arrange elements strategically, using size, contrast, and positioning to direct focus. Highlight the most important aspects and lead the viewer's eye through the content in a logical and engaging manner.

- **Embrace Creativity:** To stand out in a saturated digital landscape, embrace your creativity. Experiment with different design techniques, layouts, and innovative ideas. Find unique ways to present information or tell a story through visuals. Don't be afraid to take risks and think outside the box to create visually captivating content that leaves a lasting impression.

- **Incorporate Visual Storytelling**: Humans are wired to connect with stories. Use visual storytelling techniques to engage your audience and create a narrative around your content. Whether it's through sequential images, animations, or interactive elements, storytelling adds depth and intrigue to your visuals.

- **Optimize for Different Platforms:** Consider the platforms where your visual content will be shared. Each platform has its own specifications and requirements. Adapt your visuals accordingly to ensure they display properly and retain their impact across different devices and screen sizes.

- **Keep it Simple and Concise**: In today's fast-paced world, attention spans are shorter than ever. Keep your visual content simple, concise, and easily digestible. Avoid clutter and excessive elements that may distract or overwhelm your audience. A clean and minimalist approach can often be more powerful.

- **Test and Analyze**: Finally, don't forget to test and analyze the performance of your visual content. Monitor metrics such as engagement, click-through rates, and conversion rates to understand what resonates best with your audience. Use these insights to refine your approach and continually improve the captivating power of your visuals.

By applying these principles and strategies, you can create captivating visual content that grabs attention, sparks emotions, and drives meaningful connections with your audience. Remember to stay authentic to your brand and consistently evaluate the effectiveness of your visuals to stay ahead in the ever-evolving visual landscape.

6.3 Instagram Influencer Marketing

Instagram influencer marketing is a type of social media marketing that uses influencers to promote a brand or product to their followers. Influencers are people who have built a large and engaged following on Instagram, and they are often seen as experts in their field. When an influencer recommends a product or service, their followers are more likely to trust and purchase it.

There are many benefits to using Instagram influencer marketing.

First, it can help you reach a wider audience. Influencers have access to a large number of followers, and they can help you get your brand in front of people who might not otherwise know about it.

Second, influencer marketing can help you build trust with your target audience. When people see that their favorite influencers are using and recommending your products, they are more likely to trust you and your brand. Third, influencer marketing can help you increase sales. When people see that their favorite influencers are using and recommending your products, they are more likely to purchase them.

If you're thinking about using Instagram influencer marketing, there are a few things you need to keep in mind.

First, you need to choose the right influencers. Not all influencers are created equal. You need to find influencers who have a large and engaged following, and who are relevant to your target audience.

Second, you need to create a clear brief. When you work with an influencer, you need to be clear about what you want them to do. You need to provide them with the content you want them to post, as well as the hashtags and other details.

Third, you need to track your results. It's important to track the results of your influencer marketing campaigns so that you can see what's working and what's not. You can track things like website traffic, sales, and brand awareness.

Instagram influencer marketing can be a great way to reach a wider audience, build trust with your target audience, and increase sales. However, it's important to choose the right influencers, create a clear brief, and track your results. If you do these things, you can be sure that your influencer marketing campaigns will be successful.

Here are some tips for creating a successful influencer marketing campaign:

Choose influencers who are relevant to your target audience.

Create a clear brief that outlines what you want the influencer to do.

Provide the influencer with the content you want them to post, as well as the hashtags and other details.

Track your results so that you can see what's working and what's not.

If you follow these tips, you can be sure that your influencer marketing campaigns will be successful.

Engaging Audiences with Twitter

7.1 Crafting Engaging Tweets

Twitter is a powerful social media platform that can be used to connect with your audience, share your thoughts and ideas, and drive traffic to your website or blog. But how do you make sure your tweets are engaging and get noticed?

Here are a few tips:

Keep it short and sweet. Twitter only allows 280 characters per tweet, so make sure your messages are concise and to the point.

Use visuals. Tweets with images or videos get more engagement than those without.

Ask questions. Asking questions is a great way to start a conversation and get people involved.

Use hashtags. Hashtags are a great way to categorize your tweets and make them more discoverable.

Be timely. Tweeting about current events or trends is a great way to get people's attention.

Be yourself. People can spot a fake from a mile away, so be yourself and let your personality shine through in your tweets.

Here are some examples of engaging tweets:

"New blog post up! Check out my thoughts on [topic]."

"What's your favorite [thing]? Tweet me and let me know!"

"I'm giving away a free [item] to one of my followers! RT this tweet to enter."

"Just saw [celebrity] at [event]! #fangirlmoment"

"It's [holiday]! What are you doing to celebrate?"

By following these tips, you can craft engaging tweets that will help you connect with your audience and grow your following.

Here are some additional tips for crafting engaging tweets:

Use humor. People love to laugh, so use humor in your tweets to make them more engaging.

Be positive. People are more likely to engage with tweets that are positive and upbeat.

Be creative. Don't be afraid to experiment with different types of tweets to see what works best for your audience.

Be consistent. Tweet regularly to keep your audience engaged.

By following these tips, you can craft engaging tweets that will help you reach your marketing goals.

7.2 Using Hashtags and Trending Topics

Hashtags and trending topics are a great way to connect with people on Twitter. They can help you find people who are interested in the same things as you, and they can help you get your message seen by a wider audience.

How to use hashtags

To use a hashtag, simply type the # symbol followed by a word or phrase. For example, if you're talking about Twitter, you might use the hashtag #twitter.

You can use hashtags anywhere in your tweet, but they're most effective when they're used at the beginning of your tweet. This is because hashtags are indexed by Twitter, so when someone searches for a hashtag, your tweet will show up in the results.

You can use as many hashtags as you want, but it's best to use no more than two or three per tweet. Too many hashtags can make your tweet look spammy.

How to find trending topics

Twitter has a built-in trending section that you can use to find popular topics. To access the trending section, click on the "Explore" tab and then click on the "Trending" tab.

The trending section will show you a list of the top trending topics in your region. You can also view trending topics in other regions by changing your location.

How to use trending topics

Once you've found a trending topic, you can use it to connect with people who are interested in the same thing as you. You can tweet about the topic, retweet other people's tweets about the topic, or reply to other people's tweets about the topic.

Using trending topics is a great way to get your message seen by a wider audience. It's also a great way to connect with people who are interested in the same things as you.

Here are some tips for using hashtags and trending topics:

Use relevant hashtags. When choosing hashtags, make sure they're relevant to the content of your tweet. This will help you reach people who are actually interested in what you have to say.

Don't use too many hashtags. As mentioned above, it's best to use no more than two or three hashtags per tweet. Too many hashtags can make your tweet look spammy.

Keep an eye on trending topics. Trending topics are a great way to find new people to connect with. Be sure to check the trending section regularly to see what's popular.

Using hashtags and trending topics is a great way to get the most out of Twitter. By following these tips, you can use hashtags and trending topics to connect with people, share your message, and grow your audience.

7.3 Twitter Advertising and Analytics

Twitter Advertising and Analytics

Twitter is a powerful platform for businesses to reach their target audiences. With over 330 million active users, Twitter offers a unique opportunity to connect with people who are already interested in what you have to offer.

Twitter Advertising can help you reach your target audience with relevant content. You can choose to target your ads based on demographics, interests, and even keywords. This means that you can be sure that your ads are being seen by people who are most likely to be interested in what you have to offer.

Twitter Analytics can help you track the performance of your Twitter campaigns. You can see how many people have seen your ads, how many people have clicked on your links, and even how many people have converted into customers. This information can help you optimize your campaigns and get better results.

If you're looking for a way to reach your target audience and track the performance of your campaigns, Twitter Advertising and Analytics are a great option.

Here are some of the benefits of using Twitter Advertising and Analytics:

Reach a large and engaged audience

Target your ads based on demographics, interests, and keywords

Track the performance of your campaigns

Get insights into your audience

Improve your Twitter content strategy

If you're not already using Twitter Advertising and Analytics, I encourage you to give them a try. They can be a valuable tool for businesses of all sizes.

Here are some tips for using Twitter Advertising and Analytics effectively:

Set clear goals for your campaigns. What do you want to achieve with your Twitter advertising? Do you want to increase brand awareness, drive traffic to your website, or generate leads?

Target your ads to the right audience. Use Twitter's targeting options to reach people who are most likely to be interested in what you have to offer.

Track the performance of your campaigns. Use Twitter Analytics to see how many people have seen your ads, how many people have clicked on your links, and even how many people have converted into customers.

Use the insights you gain to improve your Twitter content

strategy. Use the data from Twitter Analytics to learn what content your audience is interested in and how you can better engage with them.

Twitter Advertising and Analytics can be a powerful tool for businesses of all sizes. By following these tips, you can use them to reach your target audience, track the performance of your campaigns, and improve your Twitter content strategy.

Harnessing the Power of LinkedIn

8.1 Building a Strong LinkedIn Profile

In today's professional landscape, having a strong LinkedIn profile is essential for building a successful career. LinkedIn has become the go-to platform for networking, job searching, and establishing your professional brand. By optimizing your LinkedIn profile, you can enhance your online presence, attract potential employers or clients, and open doors to new opportunities. Here are some key tips to help you build a strong LinkedIn profile:

Profile Picture and Background Photo:

Choose a professional, high-quality headshot for your profile picture. Ensure that you are well-dressed and have a friendly yet confident expression. Additionally, consider adding a background photo that reflects your industry or professional interests, such as a relevant work environment or industry-related image.

Compelling Headline and Summary:

Craft a compelling headline that showcases your expertise and unique value proposition. It should be concise, attention-grabbing, and keyword-rich. Your summary should provide an overview of your professional background, highlight your key accomplishments, and convey your career goals. Use this section to showcase your skills, experiences, and aspirations.

Detailed Work Experience:

List your work experience in reverse chronological order, starting with your current or most recent position. Include relevant details about your responsibilities, achievements, and the impact you made in each role. Use action verbs and quantify your achievements whenever possible. Consider including recommendations from colleagues or supervisors to add credibility to your profile.

Skills and Endorsements:

Select and list your key skills to highlight your areas of expertise. Be strategic and focus on skills that are relevant to your career goals. Connect with colleagues, former classmates, and industry professionals who can endorse your skills. Endorsements provide social proof and can enhance your professional credibility.

Education and Certifications:

Include your educational background, including degrees, certifications, and any relevant coursework. Highlight any honors, awards, or extracurricular activities that demonstrate your commitment and excellence. This section helps establish your academic foundation and showcases your dedication to continuous learning.

Engage in Content Creation:

Publish and share insightful and relevant content on LinkedIn to demonstrate your expertise and thought leadership. This can include articles, industry news, or your own original insights. Engage with other professionals by commenting on their posts and participating in relevant discussions. Consistently sharing valuable content helps you build a reputation as a knowledgeable professional.

Grow Your Network:

Actively connect with professionals in your industry, colleagues, classmates, and other individuals who align with your career interests. Personalize your connection requests by mentioning how you know or admire the person. Engaging with your connections by congratulating them on their achievements, sharing their content, or offering assistance can strengthen your professional relationships.

Recommendations and Endorsements:

Request recommendations from colleagues, supervisors, or clients who can provide genuine testimonials about your skills and work ethic. These recommendations carry weight and can enhance your credibility. Return the favor by writing recommendations for others in your network. Similarly, endorse the skills of your connections to foster a reciprocal relationship.

Utilize Multimedia and Projects:

LinkedIn allows you to showcase your work through multimedia presentations, images, documents, or videos. If applicable, include samples of your work or projects you have completed. This visual representation provides a more comprehensive view of your abilities and adds depth to your profile.

Regularly Update and Maintain Your Profile:

Keep your LinkedIn profile up to date with your latest experiences, accomplishments, and skills. Share your career milestones, promotions, and new certifications. Stay active on the platform by engaging with your connections, joining relevant groups, and participating in professional discussions.

Remember, building a strong LinkedIn profile is an ongoing process. Regularly review and refine your profile to ensure it accurately represents your professional brand. By investing time and effort into optimizing your LinkedIn presence, you can attract valuable connections and opportunities.

8.2 Leveraging LinkedIn Groups and Communities

LinkedIn Groups and Communities have become powerful tools for professionals to connect, network, and share industry insights. Leveraging these groups effectively can significantly enhance your professional presence, expand your network, and unlock numerous opportunities. Whether you are a job seeker, a business professional, or an industry expert, LinkedIn Groups and Communities offer a wealth of resources and engagement possibilities.

- **Join Relevant Groups:** Start by identifying groups that align with your professional interests, career goals, and industry. Look for active groups with a substantial number of members and discussions. Joining these groups enables you to connect with like-minded professionals, share your expertise, and learn from others in your field. Aim for a balance between larger, more general groups and niche-specific communities to maximize your networking potential.

- **Engage and Contribute**: Actively participate in group discussions by sharing your insights, asking thoughtful questions, and offering valuable advice. Engaging in meaningful conversations not only establishes you as an industry expert but also helps you build connections with other group members. Remember to be respectful, professional, and authentic in your interactions.

- **Share Valuable Content**: Share relevant articles, blog posts, industry news, or thought-provoking content with your LinkedIn Groups. This positions you as a knowledgeable resource within the community and sparks discussions around your expertise. Ensure that the content you share adds value and is aligned with the group's interests and guidelines.

- **Start Discussions**: Take the initiative to start discussions within the groups you belong to. Pose open-ended questions, seek input on industry trends or challenges, or share interesting case studies. This helps foster engagement, encourages others to share their perspectives, and boosts your visibility as a thought leader.

- **Network and Connect:** LinkedIn Groups are an excellent platform to expand your professional network. Take the opportunity to connect with individuals who actively contribute to group discussions and whose expertise aligns with your interests. Personalize your connection requests to establish a meaningful connection and mention your shared group membership.

- **Create Your Own Group**: If you have a specific area of expertise or a targeted niche, consider creating your own LinkedIn Group. This allows you to cultivate a community centered around your professional interests, establish yourself as a thought leader, and attract relevant professionals to engage and network with. Manage your group actively, facilitate discussions, and provide valuable resources to keep members engaged.

- **Leverage Group Recommendations**: LinkedIn Groups often serve as a platform for professionals to seek recommendations and referrals. Keep an eye on such requests and, when appropriate, offer your assistance or suggest relevant connections. Being helpful and supportive in these instances can strengthen your reputation and foster reciprocity within the group.

- **Monitor Group Notifications**: Stay updated with the activities and discussions in your LinkedIn

Groups by adjusting your notification settings. Regularly check the group updates, respond to comments on your posts, and engage with other members' content. Consistency and active participation are key to maximizing the benefits of these groups.

Remember to respect the guidelines and rules set by each group, as spamming or self-promotion can harm your professional reputation. By leveraging LinkedIn Groups and Communities effectively, you can enhance your professional network, gain valuable insights, and position yourself as a trusted authority in your industry.

8.3 LinkedIn Advertising and Lead Generation

LinkedIn, the world's largest professional networking platform, offers a powerful advertising and lead generation platform for businesses. With its vast user base of professionals and robust targeting options, LinkedIn has become a go-to platform for B2B (business-to-business) marketers looking to reach their target audience and generate high-quality leads. In this article, we will explore the benefits and strategies of LinkedIn advertising and lead generation.

- **Targeted Reach**: One of the key advantages of LinkedIn advertising is its ability to reach a highly targeted audience. LinkedIn allows you to target users based on various criteria such as industry, job title, company size, seniority, and more. This level of granularity ensures that your ads are displayed to the right professionals who are more likely to be interested in your products or services.

- **Professional Environment**: LinkedIn provides a professional environment where users are actively seeking business-related content and opportunities. This context makes it an ideal platform for B2B marketers to engage with professionals who are more receptive to business-focused messages. Whether you are looking to promote a new product, drive website traffic, or generate leads, LinkedIn offers a conducive environment to achieve your marketing goals.

- **Sponsored Content**: LinkedIn offers several ad formats, with sponsored content being the most popular. Sponsored content appears directly in users' news feeds, seamlessly blending in with organic content. This native advertising approach increases the chances of engagement and allows you to deliver your message in a non-intrusive manner. You can include compelling visuals, videos, and relevant links to drive traffic to your website or landing page.

- **Lead Generation Forms**: LinkedIn's lead generation forms simplify the process of capturing leads from your ads. When users click on your ad, a pre-filled form appears with their LinkedIn profile information. This convenience encourages users to submit their details, making it easier for you to collect high-quality leads. You can customize the form fields to gather specific information that aligns with your lead nurturing process.

- **InMail Advertising**: InMail is LinkedIn's messaging feature that allows you to send personalized messages to LinkedIn users who are not your connections. InMail ads can be highly effective for lead generation, especially when combined with targeted audience segmentation. Crafting compelling and personalized messages that resonate with the recipients can result in higher response rates and lead conversions.

- **Remarketing Opportunities**: LinkedIn also provides remarketing capabilities, allowing you to re-engage users who have previously interacted with your ads or website. By installing the LinkedIn Insight Tag on your website, you can track website visitors and create custom audiences for remarketing campaigns. This feature enables you to stay top-of-mind with potential leads and nurture them through the sales funnel.

- **Detailed Analytics**: LinkedIn's advertising platform provides comprehensive analytics and reporting tools to measure the performance of your campaigns. You can track key metrics such as impressions, clicks, engagement, leads generated, and more. These insights allow you to optimize your campaigns in real-time, making data-driven decisions to improve your ROI (return on investment).

In conclusion, LinkedIn advertising and lead generation offer significant opportunities for businesses to connect with a highly targeted professional audience. By leveraging the platform's robust targeting options, native ad formats, lead generation forms, and remarketing capabilities, you can effectively drive brand awareness, generate quality leads, and achieve your marketing objectives. LinkedIn's analytics tools also provide valuable insights to optimize your campaigns and maximize your advertising investment.

Consider integrating LinkedIn into your B2B marketing strategy to unlock its potential and reach a valuable audience of professionals.

Creating Compelling Video Content on YouTube

9.1 YouTube Channel Setup and Optimization

Setting up and optimizing a YouTube channel is essential for maximizing your reach and engagement with your audience. Whether you're a content creator, a business, or an organization, a well-structured and optimized channel can help you stand out in the crowded digital landscape. Here are some key steps to consider when setting up and optimizing your YouTube channel:

Channel Creation:

Sign in to YouTube using your Google account or create a new account.

Click on your profile picture and select "Create a channel" or "Your channel."

Choose a name for your channel that reflects your brand or content niche.

Customize your channel art (banner) and profile picture to create a visually appealing and recognizable brand identity.

Channel Layout:

Organize your channel's homepage by creating sections and playlists.

Highlight your best content and categorize videos into relevant playlists.

Rearrange the sections to showcase featured videos or series prominently.

Enable the channel trailer feature to introduce new visitors to your content.

Channel Optimization:

Craft a compelling channel description that clearly explains what your channel offers.

Incorporate relevant keywords in your channel description and video titles to improve searchability.

Add links to your website, social media profiles, and other relevant platforms in the channel banner or About section.

Enable channel tags to help YouTube understand your channel's content and improve recommendations.

Video Production:

Invest in quality equipment, such as a good camera, microphone, and lighting setup, to produce high-quality videos.

Plan your content in advance and create a production schedule to ensure regular uploads.

Edit your videos to enhance visual appeal, remove mistakes, and maintain a consistent style.

Optimize video titles, descriptions, and tags with relevant keywords to increase discoverability.

Audience Engagement:

Encourage viewers to like, comment, and share your videos to increase engagement.

Respond to comments and interact with your audience to foster a sense of community.

Utilize YouTube's community features, such as community posts, polls, and live chats, to engage with your audience further.

Collaborate with other YouTubers or influencers to expand your reach and tap into new audiences.

Analytics and Optimization:

Utilize YouTube Analytics to gain insights into your audience demographics, watch time, and engagement metrics.

Analyze your top-performing videos and identify patterns or trends to inform future content creation.

Experiment with different video formats, lengths, and topics based on audience feedback and analytics.

Stay up-to-date with YouTube's algorithm changes and best practices to optimize your channel's visibility and discoverability.

Remember, building a successful YouTube channel takes time and dedication. Consistently delivering high-quality content, engaging with your audience, and staying informed about trends and strategies will help you grow your channel and achieve your goals.

9.2 Video Production Tips and Techniques

Video production is an art that combines technical expertise, creativity, and effective storytelling. Whether you're a beginner or an experienced videographer, understanding essential tips and techniques can elevate the quality of your videos. From pre-production planning to post-production editing, here are some valuable insights to enhance your video production skills.

- **Define your objectives**: Before starting any video project, clearly define your goals and objectives. Understand the purpose of the video, whether it's to inform, entertain, or educate your audience. Having a clear vision will guide your decision-making process throughout production.

- **Plan your shots**: Storyboarding and shot lists are invaluable tools for planning your video. Create a visual roadmap that outlines each shot, camera angle, and sequence. This will help you stay organized and ensure that you capture all the necessary footage.

- **Lighting is key**: Good lighting can make a significant difference in the quality of your video. Utilize natural light whenever possible, but also consider using artificial lighting equipment like softboxes or LED panels to achieve a well-lit scene. Experiment with different lighting setups to create the desired mood and ambiance.

- **Capture high-quality audio**: Poor audio can ruin an otherwise excellent video. Invest in a good microphone, such as a shotgun or lavalier microphone, to capture clear and crisp audio. Minimize background noise and monitor audio levels throughout the recording process to ensure optimal sound quality.

- **Use stable camera techniques**: Shaky footage is distracting and unprofessional. Invest in a tripod or a stabilizer to keep your camera steady. Additionally, learn and practice proper handheld camera techniques to maintain stability while filming moving shots.

- **Composition and framing**: Consider the rule of thirds, leading lines, and other compositional techniques to create visually appealing shots. Pay attention to the placement of your subject within the frame and think about how each element contributes to the overall composition.

- **Experiment with camera movements**: Static shots can be visually monotonous. Explore different camera movements, such as panning, tilting, and tracking, to add dynamism to your videos. These techniques can help guide the viewer's attention and create a more engaging viewing experience.

- **Edit strategically**: Effective editing can transform raw footage into a polished final product. Be selective with your shots and trim out any unnecessary content. Use transitions, effects, and music to enhance the storytelling and maintain a cohesive flow. Experiment with pacing and timing to create a captivating narrative.

- **Color grading**: Color grading is the process of adjusting and enhancing the colors in your video. It can significantly impact the overall mood and atmosphere. Experiment with different color grading techniques to achieve the desired aesthetic and convey the intended emotions.

- **Continuously learn and improve:** Video production is a constantly evolving field. Stay updated with the latest trends, techniques, and equipment. Engage with online communities, attend workshops, and seek feedback to refine your skills and expand your creative horizons.

Remember, practice makes perfect. The more you experiment, learn from your mistakes, and refine your techniques, the better your video production skills will become. So, grab your camera, unleash your creativity, and start producing captivating videos that leave a lasting impact on your audience.

9.3 YouTube Advertising Strategies

YouTube advertising is a powerful tool for businesses and content creators to reach a massive audience and promote their products, services, or brand. With billions of users and a wide range of targeting options, YouTube offers various advertising strategies to help you effectively engage with your target audience. Here are some key strategies to consider when planning your YouTube advertising campaigns:

- **Pre-roll Ads:** Pre-roll ads are short video ads that appear before a user watches their chosen video content. These ads can be skipped after a few seconds, but they provide an excellent opportunity to capture viewers' attention right at the beginning. To maximize their impact, make sure your pre-roll ads are concise, engaging, and relevant to the viewer's interests.

- **In-Stream Ads**: In-stream ads are video ads that play during breaks in longer YouTube videos. They can appear in the middle of the video or at the end. These ads can be skippable or non-skippable, depending on the ad format you choose. Skippable ads give viewers the option to skip the ad after a few seconds, while non-skippable ads require viewers to watch the full ad. Consider using a combination of skippable and non-skippable ads based on your campaign objectives.

- **Display Ads**: Display ads on YouTube are static or animated image ads that appear beside the video content or on the YouTube homepage. These ads are less intrusive than video ads but can still grab viewers' attention. They can be an effective way to promote your brand or a specific product visually. Ensure your display ads are visually appealing and include a clear call to action to encourage viewers to click through to your website or landing page.

- **Video Remarketing**: YouTube allows you to create remarketing lists based on viewers' engagement with your videos or YouTube channel. This strategy enables you to target viewers who have already shown an interest in your content. By creating tailored ads for these audiences, you can reinforce your brand message and encourage them to take the next desired action, such as making a purchase or subscribing to your channel.

- **Influencer Collaborations**: Collaborating with popular YouTube influencers or content creators who have a significant following in your target market can amplify your brand's reach and credibility. Identify influencers whose content aligns with your brand values and target audience. By partnering with them, you can tap into their existing audience and benefit from their influence and expertise.

- **TrueView Discovery Ads**: TrueView discovery ads appear in the YouTube search results, related videos, or on the YouTube homepage. These ads consist of a thumbnail image and text and can drive targeted traffic to your YouTube channel or specific videos. Optimize your thumbnail and headline to make them compelling and curiosity-inducing, encouraging users to click and explore your content further.

- **Targeting Options**: YouTube offers various targeting options to help you reach your desired audience effectively. You can target based on demographics, interests, search keywords, topics, and even specific YouTube channels. By refining your targeting, you can ensure that your ads are shown to the most relevant viewers, maximizing their impact and minimizing wasted ad spend.

- **A/B Testing and Optimization**: Like any advertising campaign, it's essential to continuously test and optimize your YouTube ads. Experiment with different ad formats, creative elements, targeting options, and calls to action to identify what resonates best with your audience. Monitor key metrics such as click-through rates, view rates, and conversion rates to gauge the effectiveness of your campaigns and make data-driven improvements.

Remember, YouTube advertising is not a one-size-fits-all approach. It's crucial to understand your target audience, set clear campaign objectives, and tailor your strategies accordingly. By leveraging the various ad formats and targeting options available, you can create compelling and engaging YouTube ad campaigns that drive brand awareness, increase conversions, and ultimately achieve your marketing goals.

Part III

Advanced Strategies for Rapid Growth

10. Influencer Marketing and Collaborations

Influencer marketing and collaborations are strategies used by brands and businesses to leverage the reach and influence of social media influencers to promote their products or services. It involves partnering with influencers who have a significant following and influence in a specific niche or industry to create content that showcases or endorses the brand.

Here are some key points about influencer marketing and collaborations:

- **Definition:** Influencer marketing is a form of marketing that focuses on using influential individuals to promote a brand's products or services to their audience. Collaborations refer to partnerships between brands and influencers to create content together.

- **Types of influencers**: Influencers can be categorized based on their follower count and reach. They range from macro-influencers (with hundreds of thousands to millions of followers) to micro-influencers (with a smaller but highly engaged following) and nano-influencers (with a smaller following but strong influence in a specific niche).

- **Benefits for brands**: Influencer marketing allows brands to tap into the trust and credibility that influencers have built with their audience. It can help increase brand awareness, reach a targeted audience, drive engagement and conversions, and improve brand perception and reputation.

Choosing the right influencers: Brands should consider various factors when selecting influencers for collaborations, including their niche, target audience alignment, engagement rates, authenticity, and previous brand partnerships. It's crucial to find influencers whose values and aesthetic align with the brand's image.

- **Types of collaborations**: Collaborations can take different forms, such as sponsored posts, product reviews, giveaways, brand ambassadorships, guest blogging, influencer takeovers, and co-creating content. The specific format and deliverables depend on the brand's goals and the influencer's expertise.

- **Transparency and disclosure:** Transparency is vital in influencer marketing. Influencers are required to disclose their relationships with brands and clearly indicate when content is sponsored or a collaboration. This helps maintain trust with their audience and comply with advertising guidelines and regulations.

- **Measuring success:** Brands can measure the success of influencer marketing campaigns through various metrics, such as engagement rates, reach, impressions, website traffic, conversions, and brand sentiment analysis. Setting clear goals and tracking relevant metrics is crucial for evaluating the campaign's effectiveness.

- **Emerging trends:** The influencer marketing landscape is continuously evolving. Some emerging trends include the rise of micro- and nano-influencers, the use of user-generated content, influencer marketplaces and platforms, long-term partnerships, and a focus on authenticity and storytelling.

It's important for brands to approach influencer marketing and collaborations strategically, ensuring alignment with their overall marketing objectives and selecting influencers who can effectively represent their brand and resonate with their target audience.

10.2 Developing Successful Influencer Partnerships

Developing successful influencer partnerships requires careful planning, strategic approach, and effective execution. Here are some key steps to follow when building influencer partnerships:

- **Set Clear Objectives**: Define your goals and objectives for the influencer partnership. Are you looking to increase brand awareness, drive sales, or reach a specific target audience? Establishing clear objectives will help you select the right influencers and measure the success of your partnership.

- **Identify Relevant Influencers**: Research and identify influencers who align with your brand values, target audience, and industry. Look for influencers with a genuine and engaged following, as well as those who have previously collaborated with brands in your niche. Analyze their content, engagement rates, audience demographics, and authenticity.

- **Establish Authenticity and Fit**: Authenticity is crucial in influencer marketing. Ensure that the influencer's values, tone, and content style resonate with your brand. An authentic partnership will be more likely to resonate with the influencer's audience and generate meaningful results for your brand.

- **Build Relationships**: Take the time to build relationships with influencers before approaching them for a partnership. Engage with their content, leave thoughtful comments, and share their posts. This helps to establish a connection and increases the chances of a successful collaboration.

- **Negotiate Partnership Terms**: When reaching out to influencers, clearly communicate your expectations, deliverables, and compensation. Be open to negotiation, as influencers may have their own preferences and rates. Ensure that both parties are aligned on the scope of work, timeline, and any contractual agreements.

- **Create Authentic and Engaging Content**: Collaborate with influencers to create content that aligns with your brand message and resonates with their audience. Give influencers creative freedom while guiding them to integrate your brand naturally. The content should be engaging, informative, and authentic to maximize its impact.

- **Track and Measure Results**: Establish key performance indicators (KPIs) to measure the success of your influencer partnerships. Track metrics such as reach, engagement, website traffic, conversions, and sales. Use tracking tools and unique referral codes or links to attribute results accurately to the influencer's efforts.

- **Maintain Long-Term Relationships**: Building long-term relationships with influencers can be beneficial for sustained brand exposure and credibility. Provide timely feedback and support, collaborate on multiple campaigns, and consider ambassador programs to deepen the partnership.

- **Stay Compliant and Transparent**: Ensure that influencers comply with relevant advertising and disclosure guidelines, such as disclosing sponsored content. Transparent and compliant partnerships help maintain trust with the influencer's audience and avoid potential legal issues.

- **Learn and Iterate**: Continuously analyze the results and learn from each influencer partnership. Understand what worked well and what can be improved for future collaborations. Adapt your strategies based on the insights gained to refine your influencer marketing approach.

Remember that successful influencer partnerships are built on mutual trust, authenticity, and value exchange. By following these steps and continuously refining your approach, you can develop impactful influencer collaborations that benefit both your brand and the influencers involved.

10.3 Measuring the Impact of Influencer Marketing

Measuring the impact of influencer marketing can be crucial in evaluating the effectiveness and return on investment (ROI) of your marketing efforts. Here are some key metrics and methods commonly used to measure the impact of influencer marketing campaigns:

- **Reach:** Assess the size of the influencer's audience and the potential number of people who were exposed to your brand message or content. This can be measured by the influencer's follower count or the number of views, impressions, or reach generated by their posts.

- **Engagement:** Analyze the level of engagement your influencer content receives, such as likes, comments, shares, and saves. High engagement indicates that the content resonated with the audience and encouraged them to interact with it.

- **Conversions:** Track the number of conversions or actions taken by users as a result of the influencer's promotion. This could include purchases, sign-ups, downloads, or any other specific goals you have set for your campaign. Assigning unique tracking links or discount codes to the influencer's content can help attribute conversions directly to their efforts.

- **Website Traffic:** Monitor the amount of traffic driven to your website from the influencer's posts. Tools like Google Analytics can provide insights into the number of visitors, page views, and referral sources associated with the influencer's campaign.

- **Brand Mentions and Sentiment Analysis:** Monitor social media platforms, blogs, and other online channels for brand mentions related to your influencer campaign. Assess the sentiment of these mentions to determine if they are positive, negative, or neutral, and gauge the overall perception of your brand.

- **Cost per Engagement or Conversion**: Calculate the cost-effectiveness of your influencer marketing campaign by dividing the total campaign cost by the number of engagements or conversions generated. This metric helps you compare the relative performance of different influencers or campaigns.

- **Surveys and Feedback:** Conduct surveys or collect feedback from your target audience to gauge their awareness, perception, and recall of your influencer campaign. This qualitative data can provide valuable insights into the impact and effectiveness of the campaign beyond quantitative metrics.

- **Long-Term Brand Impact**: Consider the long-term effects of influencer marketing, such as brand awareness, brand loyalty, and customer lifetime value. While these metrics may be harder to measure immediately, they are important indicators of the overall impact of influencer marketing on your business.

Remember that the choice of metrics will depend on your campaign goals and objectives. It's essential to establish clear goals and align your measurement strategy accordingly. Additionally, using a combination of quantitative and qualitative methods will provide a more comprehensive understanding of the impact of your influencer marketing efforts.

Social Media Analytics and Data-Driven Insights

11.1   Tracking and Analyzing Social Media Metrics

Tracking and analyzing social media metrics is crucial for understanding the performance and impact of your social media campaigns. By monitoring these metrics, you can gain valuable insights into your audience, content effectiveness, and overall social media strategy. Here are some key steps to help you track and analyze social media metrics effectively:

- **Define your goals**: Before diving into tracking metrics, clearly define your social media goals. Are you aiming to increase brand awareness, drive website traffic, generate leads, or engage with your audience? Your goals will determine which metrics are most relevant for tracking.

- **Identify key metrics**: Based on your goals, determine the key metrics you need to track. Here are some common social media metrics to consider:

- **Reach and Impressions**: The number of unique users who have seen your content (reach) and the total number of times your content has been displayed (impressions).

- **Engagement:** Likes, comments, shares, and retweets indicate how well your audience is interacting with your content.

- **Follower Growth**: Monitor the growth of your social media followers over time.

- **Click-through Rate (CTR)**: The percentage of users who clicked on a link in your post.

- **Conversion Rate**: The percentage of users who completed a desired action (e.g., signing up for a newsletter, making a purchase) after clicking a link.

- **Sentiment Analysis**: Analyze the sentiment (positive, negative, neutral) of comments and mentions related to your brand.

- **Customer Lifetime Value (CLTV):** Track the value generated by customers acquired through social media.

- **Social Media Referral Traffic**: Measure the amount of traffic driven to your website from social media platforms.

- **Use analytics tools**: Social media platforms often provide built-in analytics tools that offer valuable insights. For example, Facebook Insights, Twitter Analytics, and Instagram Insights provide data on reach, engagement, follower growth, and demographics. Additionally, there are third-party tools like Google Analytics, Hootsuite, and Sprout Social that can integrate with multiple platforms and provide more comprehensive analytics.

- **Set up tracking and reporting**: Implement tracking mechanisms, such as UTM parameters, to measure the effectiveness of your social media campaigns. These parameters allow you to identify the source of traffic and conversions in your website analytics. Regularly monitor and record your metrics in a centralized reporting system, whether it's a spreadsheet or a dedicated analytics dashboard.

- **Analyze and interpret the data**: Once you have collected sufficient data, analyze the metrics to gain insights. Look for trends, patterns, and correlations between different metrics. Identify what's working and what's not, and adjust your social media strategy accordingly. For example, if you notice that video posts on Instagram receive higher engagement than images, consider focusing more on video content.

- **Iterate and optimize:** Social media metrics provide a feedback loop that allows you to continually refine your strategy. Use the insights gained from your analysis to optimize your content, posting frequency, targeting, and overall social media approach.

Remember, while metrics are important, it's also essential to align them with your broader business objectives and consider the qualitative aspects of your social media efforts, such as brand sentiment and customer feedback.

11.2   Social Media Listening and Sentiment Analysis

Social media listening and sentiment analysis are two important techniques used in analyzing and understanding the conversations and opinions shared on social media platforms.

Social media listening, also known as social media monitoring or social media intelligence, involves the process of monitoring and tracking social media channels for specific keywords, mentions, or conversations related to a brand, product, service, or topic. It allows businesses and individuals to gain insights into what people are saying about them or their areas of interest on social media.

There are various tools and software available that can help in social media listening by aggregating and organizing data from different social media platforms such as Twitter, Facebook, Instagram, and LinkedIn. These tools can capture real-time conversations, hashtags, posts, comments, and other relevant content related to the specified keywords or topics.

Sentiment analysis, on the other hand, is a technique used to analyze and determine the sentiment or opinion expressed in a piece of text, such as a social media post, review, or comment. The goal of sentiment analysis is to classify the text as positive, negative, or neutral, and sometimes even more specific emotions such as happiness, sadness, anger, or surprise.

Sentiment analysis typically involves natural language processing (NLP) techniques, including machine learning and text mining. Machine learning algorithms are trained on large datasets of labeled text to recognize patterns and sentiment cues. These algorithms can then be applied to new text data to classify the sentiment.

Businesses and organizations use social media listening and sentiment analysis for several purposes:

- **Brand monitoring:** Monitoring social media conversations helps organizations understand how their brand or product is perceived by the public. They can identify positive feedback, address negative sentiment, and take appropriate actions to improve their reputation.

- **Customer feedback and insights**: Social media provides a platform for customers to express their opinions and experiences. Analyzing sentiment allows businesses to understand customer sentiment towards their products or services, identify common issues, and make improvements accordingly.

- **Crisis management**: Social media listening can be valuable during a crisis or a PR incident. By monitoring social media conversations in real-time, organizations can identify and address negative sentiment promptly, manage public perception, and take appropriate steps to mitigate the situation.

- **Competitor analysis:** Social media listening can also provide insights into the sentiment and conversations surrounding competitors. This information can help businesses identify competitive advantages, track industry trends, and adjust their strategies accordingly.

- **Campaign evaluation**: Sentiment analysis can be used to measure the success of marketing or advertising campaigns by analyzing the sentiment expressed in social media conversations related to the campaign. It helps organizations gauge public response and make data-driven decisions for future campaigns.

Overall, social media listening and sentiment analysis provide valuable insights into public opinions, customer sentiments, and market trends. By leveraging these techniques, businesses can make informed decisions, enhance customer experiences, and optimize their strategies.

11.3 Leveraging Data for Continuous Improvement

Leveraging data for continuous improvement is a powerful strategy that businesses and organizations can adopt to enhance their operations, decision-making processes, and overall performance. It involves collecting, analyzing, and interpreting relevant data to identify areas of improvement, make data-driven decisions, and implement changes that lead to ongoing enhancements. Here are some key steps and considerations for leveraging data for continuous improvement:

- **Define goals and metrics:** Clearly define the goals and objectives you want to achieve through continuous improvement. Identify the key performance indicators (KPIs) and metrics that align with these goals. These metrics should be measurable and provide meaningful insights into the areas you want to improve.

- **Collect and organize data:** Establish data collection processes and systems to gather relevant data. This can include internal data sources (e.g., sales figures, customer feedback) and external sources (e.g., market research, industry trends). Ensure data quality and consistency by implementing data governance practices and data validation techniques.

- **Analyze and interpret data:** Use data analysis techniques to derive insights from the collected data. This can involve descriptive analytics (summarizing and visualizing data), diagnostic analytics (identifying patterns and correlations), predictive analytics (forecasting future trends), or prescriptive analytics (recommending actions based on data). Apply statistical methods, data mining, machine learning, or other advanced analytical approaches to extract valuable insights.

- **Identify improvement opportunities:** Analyze the data to identify areas where improvements can be made. Look for patterns, trends, anomalies, or bottlenecks that indicate areas for optimization. Use data visualization tools or dashboards to present the information in a clear and actionable manner.

- **Set priorities and develop action plans:** Prioritize the improvement opportunities based on their potential impact and feasibility. Develop action plans that outline the specific steps, resources, and timelines required to implement the changes. Ensure that the action plans align with your overall goals and strategic objectives.

- **Implement changes and monitor results:** Execute the

action plans and implement the identified improvements. Continuously monitor the results and measure the impact of the changes using the established metrics and KPIs. This will help you assess the effectiveness of the improvements and make any necessary adjustments.

- **Foster a data-driven culture**: Encourage a culture of data-driven decision-making within your organization. Promote the use of data and insights in discussions, planning, and problem-solving processes. Provide training and resources to employees to enhance their data literacy and analytical skills.

- **Iterate and refine:** Continuous improvement is an ongoing process. Regularly review and assess your data collection methods, analysis techniques, and improvement strategies. Adapt and refine your approach based on new data, changing circumstances, and emerging trends.

By following these steps and embracing a data-driven approach, organizations can continuously identify areas for improvement, make informed decisions, and drive ongoing enhancements in their operations, products, and services.

Social Media Advertising and Paid Campaigns

12.1 Introduction to Social Media Advertising

Social media advertising refers to the practice of promoting products, services, or brands on various social media platforms to reach a target audience. With the rise of social media platforms like Facebook, Instagram, Twitter, LinkedIn, and others, businesses and advertisers have recognized the potential of these platforms to connect with a vast number of users worldwide.

Social media advertising offers several advantages over traditional forms of advertising.

Firstly, it provides highly targeted and customizable options to reach specific demographics, interests, and behaviors of users. This level of targeting allows advertisers to deliver their messages to the right audience, increasing the chances of engagement and conversion.

Secondly, social media advertising provides opportunities for two-way communication between businesses and their target audience. Users can engage with the content, leave comments, share their opinions, and ask questions. This interaction allows businesses to build relationships, gather feedback, and address customer concerns in real-time, fostering brand loyalty and customer satisfaction.

Thirdly, social media platforms offer a wealth of data and analytics that allow advertisers to measure the effectiveness of their campaigns. Metrics such as impressions, clicks, conversions, and engagement rates provide valuable insights into the performance of ads, enabling businesses to optimize their strategies and improve their return on investment (ROI).

There are several types of social media advertising formats, including:

- **Display Ads:** These are visual ads that appear on the sidebar, in the news feed, or as banners on social media platforms. They can include images, videos, or carousels and are designed to grab the attention of users as they browse their social media feeds.

- **Sponsored Content**: This involves promoting branded content within the organic content of social media platforms. It blends seamlessly with the user's feed and appears as regular posts, but is marked as "sponsored" or "promoted."

- **Video Ads:** These are short video clips that play automatically or upon user interaction. Video ads can be highly engaging and provide an opportunity to deliver a compelling message in a dynamic format.

- **Influencer   Marketing:** Influencers are individuals with a large following on social media who can promote products or services to their audience. Influencer marketing involves collaborating with influencers to create sponsored content that promotes a brand or product.

- **Social Media Stories**: Stories have gained popularity on platforms like Instagram, Facebook, and Snapchat. These short-lived posts can include images or videos and are displayed prominently at the top of the user's feed. Advertisers can leverage this format to create immersive and interactive ads.

When developing a social media advertising strategy, it is crucial to define clear objectives, identify the target audience, select the appropriate platforms, create compelling and relevant content, and monitor and optimize the campaigns based on the available data and analytics.

Overall, social media advertising provides businesses with a powerful tool to reach and engage their target audience, increase brand awareness, drive website traffic, generate leads, and ultimately, achieve their marketing goals in an increasingly digital and connected world.

12.2 Designing Effective Ad Campaigns

Designing effective ad campaigns requires careful planning and consideration of various elements. Here are some key steps to help you create successful ad campaigns:

- **Set Clear Objectives**: Start by defining your campaign goals. Are you aiming to increase brand awareness, generate leads, drive sales, or promote a specific product/service? Clearly outlining your objectives will guide your ad campaign strategy.

- **Know Your Target Audience:** Identify your target audience and understand their demographics, interests, and needs. This knowledge will help you tailor your messages and select appropriate advertising channels to reach them effectively.

- **Craft Compelling Messages:** Develop strong and concise messaging that resonates with your target audience. Highlight the benefits of your product or service, address pain points, and create a unique selling proposition that sets you apart from competitors.

- **Choose the Right Advertising Channels**: Consider the platforms and channels that are most likely to reach your target audience. Options may include social media advertising (e.g., Facebook, Instagram, LinkedIn), search engine advertising (e.g., Google Ads), display advertising, TV/radio ads, print media, or influencer partnerships. Select channels that align with your audience demographics and campaign objectives.

- **Utilize Engaging Visuals:** Incorporate visually appealing elements into your ads. Use high-quality images, videos, or graphics that capture attention and convey your brand message effectively. Ensure that visuals are consistent with your brand identity.

- **Test and Optimize:** Conduct A/B testing to compare different ad variations and determine what works best. Experiment with different headlines, visuals, calls to action (CTAs), and ad formats to identify the most effective combination. Continuously monitor campaign performance and make data-driven adjustments to optimize results.

- **Consistency and Branding:** Maintain consistent branding across all ad campaigns to build brand recognition and trust. Use consistent color schemes, fonts, logos, and brand voice to reinforce your brand identity in all communication.

- **Personalization and Targeting:** Leverage data and customer insights to personalize your ad campaigns. Tailor messages based on user behavior, preferences, or demographics to create a more personalized experience that resonates with individuals.

- **Clear Call to Action:** Clearly state what action you want viewers to take after seeing your ad. Whether it's visiting a website, making a purchase, or signing up for a newsletter, provide a compelling and easy-to-follow call to action that encourages users to engage with your brand.

- **Track and Measure Results:** Set up tracking mechanisms to measure the effectiveness of your ad campaigns. Monitor key performance indicators (KPIs) such as click-through rates, conversion rates, impressions, and return on investment (ROI). Analyze data to gain insights, identify areas for improvement, and refine future campaigns.

Remember, designing effective ad campaigns is an iterative process. Continuously learn from your data, adapt your strategies, and refine your campaigns to achieve the best possible outcomes.

12.3 Budgeting and Optimization Strategies

Budgeting and optimization strategies are essential for managing finances effectively and maximizing resources.

Here are some key strategies you can employ:

- **Set clear financial goals:** Define your short-term and long-term financial goals. This could include saving for a down payment, paying off debt, or building an emergency fund. Having specific goals helps guide your budgeting and optimization efforts.

- **Create a budget:** Develop a comprehensive budget that outlines your income and expenses. Track your spending and categorize it to identify areas where you can cut back or optimize. Allocate funds to essential expenses first, such as housing, utilities, and debt payments, and then prioritize savings and discretionary spending.

- **Prioritize savings:** Make saving a priority in your budget. Set aside a portion of your income for savings and treat it as a non-negotiable expense. Consider automating savings by setting up automatic transfers to a separate savings account or investment vehicle.

- **Identify and reduce unnecessary expenses:** Review your expenses and identify areas where you can cut back. This could involve canceling unused subscriptions, reducing dining out, shopping smartly for groceries, or finding cost-effective alternatives for everyday expenses.

- **Track and analyze spending**: Use budgeting tools or apps to track your expenses. Analyze your spending patterns over time to identify trends, areas of overspending, or opportunities for optimization. This awareness will help you make informed decisions about your finances.

- **Optimize debt repayment:** If you have outstanding debt, develop a strategy to pay it off efficiently. Consider the snowball or avalanche method. The snowball method involves paying off the smallest debt first, while the avalanche method focuses on paying off debts with the highest interest rates first. Choose the strategy that aligns with your financial goals and motivates you to stay on track.

- **Explore ways to increase income**: Look for opportunities to boost your income. This could involve negotiating a raise, taking on freelance work or a side gig, monetizing a hobby or skill, or investing in income-generating assets. Increasing your income can provide additional resources for savings and debt repayment.

- **Review and optimize recurring expenses:** Regularly review your recurring expenses, such as insurance policies, utility bills, internet and cable plans, or mobile phone contracts. Shop around for better deals, negotiate rates with service providers, or consider switching to more cost-effective options.

- **Take advantage of discounts and rewards:** Look for discounts, coupons, and loyalty programs when making purchases. Take advantage of credit card rewards, cashback programs, or airline miles to optimize your spending. However, ensure that you use credit cards responsibly and avoid unnecessary debt.

- **Continuously evaluate and adjust:** Regularly review your budget, financial goals, and optimization strategies. Life circumstances change, and your financial priorities may shift. Stay adaptable and make adjustments as needed to ensure your budget remains effective and aligned with your goals.

Remember, budgeting and optimization strategies are highly individualized. Tailor these strategies to your specific financial situation and goals. Seek professional advice if needed and remain disciplined and consistent in your approach.

Part IV

Sustaining Growth and Adaptation

13. Social Media Crisis Management

Social media crisis management is the process of effectively handling and mitigating a crisis situation that arises on social media platforms. With the widespread use of social media, organizations and individuals are more vulnerable to public scrutiny, negative feedback, and potential reputation damage. Having a well-defined crisis management strategy is crucial to address and minimize the impact of such situations. Here are some key steps to consider for social media crisis management:

- **Monitor social media:** Implement a robust social media monitoring system to keep track of conversations, mentions, and sentiment around your brand. This will enable you to identify potential crisis situations early on.

- **Act swiftly:** Once a crisis is detected, it's important to respond quickly. Delayed or no response can escalate the situation and harm your reputation. Acknowledge the issue promptly and assure stakeholders that you are taking it seriously.

- **Gather information:** Assess the situation and gather all the necessary information before responding. Identify the root cause, understand the context, and gather relevant facts. Avoid making assumptions or speculating, as it can worsen the crisis.

- **Formulate a response strategy:** Develop a clear and concise message that addresses the issue at hand. Depending on the severity of the crisis, determine whether a public statement is necessary or if it can be addressed through private communication.

- **Choose the right channel**: Select the appropriate social media platform to respond on, considering factors such as the nature of the crisis and where the issue originated. It's important to respond directly on the platform where the crisis is unfolding to ensure your message reaches the affected audience.

- **Be transparent and honest:** In your response, be transparent about the situation and take responsibility for any mistakes or shortcomings. Honest communication can help rebuild trust and credibility.

- **Engage with stakeholders:** Engage in meaningful conversations with affected stakeholders. Respond to comments, questions, and concerns promptly and empathetically. Addressing individual concerns shows that you value your audience's opinions and are committed to resolving the issue.

- **Monitor and adapt:** Continuously monitor the situation and the response to your communication. Adjust your strategy as needed based on feedback and evolving circumstances. Stay responsive and show genuine efforts to resolve the crisis.

- **Learn from the experience:** Once the crisis is resolved, evaluate the situation and identify lessons learned. Assess what could have been done differently and implement changes to prevent similar situations in the future.

- **Develop a crisis management plan:** Proactively develop a social media crisis management plan that outlines roles, responsibilities, and procedures for handling different types of crises. Regularly review and update the plan to stay prepared.

Remember, effective social media crisis management requires a calm and calculated approach. By being proactive, transparent, and responsive, you can navigate through crisis situations and protect your brand's reputation.

13.1   Handling Negative Feedback and Reviews

Handling negative feedback and reviews can be challenging, but it's an important aspect of managing your reputation and maintaining good customer relationships. Here are some tips to help you handle negative feedback and reviews effectively:

- **Stay calm and composed**: It's natural to feel defensive or upset when receiving negative feedback, but it's important to remain calm and composed. Take a moment to gather your thoughts before responding.

- **Listen and understand**: Read or listen to the feedback carefully, trying to understand the customer's concerns or dissatisfaction. Put yourself in their shoes and try to see the situation from their perspective.

- **Don't take it personally**: Remember that negative feedback is not a personal attack on you. Separate yourself from the criticism and focus on the issue at hand.

- **Respond promptly**: Timely responses show that you value customer feedback and are committed to addressing concerns. Aim to respond within 24-48 hours, if possible.

- **Apologize and take responsibility**: Even if you believe the customer's complaint is unwarranted, offer a sincere apology for any inconvenience or dissatisfaction they experienced. Taking responsibility shows that you care about their experience.

- **Offer a solution:** Propose a solution to address the customer's concerns. If appropriate, offer a refund, a replacement, or any other form of compensation to resolve the issue. Be proactive in finding a resolution that satisfies the customer.

- **Be professional and polite**: Maintain a professional and polite tone in all your interactions. Avoid becoming defensive or engaging in arguments. Responding courteously can help defuse the situation and demonstrate your commitment to customer service.

- **Take feedback as an opportunity to improve**: Use negative feedback as a learning experience. Analyze the feedback and identify any patterns or areas for improvement in your products, services, or processes. Making necessary changes can help prevent similar issues in the future.

- **Encourage private communication**: When responding to negative feedback on public platforms, provide contact information or invite the customer to reach out privately to discuss the matter further. This shows that you are willing to address the issue directly and resolve it offline.

- **Learn from positive feedback**: Don't forget to acknowledge and appreciate positive feedback as well. Use positive reviews to identify your strengths and continue providing excellent service.

Remember, every negative review or feedback is an opportunity to improve your business and strengthen customer relationships. By handling them with professionalism and empathy, you can turn a negative experience into a positive one.

13.2   Responding to Social Media Crises

Responding to social media crises can be challenging, but it's important to handle them promptly and effectively. Here are some key steps to consider when responding to social media crises:

- **Monitor and identify the issue:** Actively monitor your social media channels and other online platforms to identify any potential crises. Pay attention to negative comments, complaints, or trending topics related to your brand or organization.

- **Assess the situation:** Once you've identified a potential crisis, assess the severity and impact it could have on your brand's reputation. Determine if it requires immediate attention or if it can be addressed through a planned response.

- **Respond quickly but thoughtfully**: In social media crises, time is of the essence. Acknowledge the issue publicly and respond promptly to show that you're aware and taking it seriously. However, avoid knee-jerk reactions and ensure your response is thoughtful and well-considered.

- **Apologize if necessary**: If your brand or organization is at fault, offer a sincere apology. Take responsibility for the situation and show empathy towards those affected. Be genuine in your apology and avoid making excuses or deflecting blame.

- **Provide accurate information**: In the midst of a crisis, misinformation can spread rapidly.

Counteract it by providing accurate and up-to-date information about the situation. This can help mitigate further damage and regain trust from your audience.

- **Take the conversation offline**: If possible, move the conversation away from the public eye and into private channels. Encourage individuals with specific concerns or complaints to reach out via direct messages or email, where you can address their issues more personally and effectively.

- **Monitor and engage with the conversation**: Continuously monitor the conversation surrounding the crisis and engage with users who have questions or concerns. Respond promptly and transparently to provide updates, clarify any misunderstandings, and demonstrate your commitment to resolving the issue.

- **Learn from the experience**: Once the crisis has subsided, take the opportunity to reflect on the situation and learn from it. Analyze what went wrong, identify areas for improvement, and implement strategies to prevent similar issues in the future.

- **Rebuild trust**: Rebuilding trust takes time and consistent effort. Demonstrate transparency, deliver on any promises made during the crisis, and consistently provide high-quality products or services. Engage with your audience positively and focus on rebuilding relationships.

Remember, each social media crisis is unique, and the appropriate response may vary depending on the circumstances. It's important to adapt these steps to fit your specific situation while keeping in mind the best practices of effective crisis communication.

13.3   Rebuilding Trust and Reputation

Rebuilding trust and reputation can be a challenging process, but it is possible with consistent effort and a genuine commitment to change. Here are some steps you can take to rebuild trust and reputation:

- **Acknowledge and take responsibility:** Begin by acknowledging any mistakes or wrongdoing that may have led to the loss of trust and reputation. Take responsibility for your actions and avoid making excuses or shifting blame.

- **Apologize sincerely:** Offer a genuine and heartfelt apology to those who have been affected. Clearly communicate that you understand the impact of your actions and express remorse for any harm caused.

- **Be transparent:** Foster trust by being open and transparent about your intentions, actions, and any changes you are making. Share information willingly and honestly, and address any concerns or questions openly.

- **Communicate consistently:** Maintain open lines of communication with stakeholders, customers, or the public. Be responsive to feedback and address any issues promptly and effectively. Consistent and clear communication demonstrates your commitment to rebuilding trust.

- **Deliver on promises:** Rebuilding trust requires following through on your commitments. Make sure you fulfill any promises or commitments you make, and strive to exceed expectations whenever possible.

- **Implement corrective measures:** Take proactive steps to rectify the situation and prevent similar issues from occurring in the future. This may involve implementing new policies, procedures, or training programs to ensure that the problems are not repeated.

- **Rebuild relationships:** Invest time and effort into rebuilding relationships with stakeholders, customers, or the public. Show genuine care and concern, and work to rebuild trust through consistent positive interactions.

- **Demonstrate consistency and reliability:** Consistency is crucial in rebuilding trust and reputation. Ensure that your actions align with your words over an extended period. Consistently meeting expectations and delivering quality work will help regain trust over time.

- **Learn from past mistakes:** Demonstrate a commitment to personal and organizational growth by learning from past mistakes. Embrace a culture of continuous improvement and use the experience as an opportunity for positive change.

- **Give it time:** Rebuilding trust and reputation is not an overnight process. It takes time, patience, and consistent effort. Be prepared for setbacks along the way, but remain dedicated to the process and show perseverance.

Remember that rebuilding trust and reputation is a journey that requires ongoing commitment and effort. By taking these steps and demonstrating consistent positive change, you can gradually rebuild trust and regain a positive reputation.

Staying Ahead with Emerging Trends

14.1 The Future of Social Media Marketing

The future of social media marketing is expected to evolve and adapt to the changing landscape of technology and consumer behavior. Here are some trends and predictions for the future of social media marketing:

- **Increased personalization:** As social media platforms gather more data on user preferences and behavior, marketers will have more opportunities to deliver personalized content and advertisements. Tailoring messages to individual users' interests and preferences will become increasingly important for effective marketing.

- **Video content domination**: Video content has already gained significant popularity on social media platforms, and this trend is expected to continue. Short-form videos, live streaming, and interactive video formats will dominate social media feeds. Marketers will need to adapt their strategies to create engaging and compelling video content to capture users' attention.

- **Influencer marketing evolution**: Influencer marketing will continue to play a significant role in social media marketing. However, there might be a shift towards micro-influencers or nano-influencers who have smaller but highly engaged and niche audiences. Authenticity, trust, and relevance will be key factors in choosing influencers for marketing campaigns.

- **Rise of augmented reality (AR) and virtual reality (VR):** AR and VR technologies are expected to become more integrated into social media platforms. Brands will leverage these immersive technologies to create interactive experiences for users, such as virtual try-on for products, virtual showrooms, or branded AR filters. This will provide new opportunities for innovative and engaging marketing campaigns.

- **Social commerce growth:** Social media platforms will continue to enhance their shopping capabilities, enabling users to make purchases without leaving the app. Features like "shoppable posts" and "buy buttons" will become more prevalent. Marketers will need to optimize their social media strategies to drive sales and conversions directly from social platforms.

- **Privacy and data protection**: With growing concerns around data privacy, social media platforms and marketers will need to ensure compliance with evolving regulations and prioritize user privacy. Marketers will need to be transparent with their data practices and seek permission-based marketing strategies to build trust with their audiences.

- **Artificial intelligence (AI) and chatbots:** AI-powered chatbots will become more sophisticated, enabling brands to provide instant customer support and personalized experiences on social media platforms. AI will also play a significant role in data analysis, ad targeting, and content recommendations, helping marketers optimize their strategies based on real-time insights.

- **Emphasis on social responsibility:** Consumers are increasingly demanding socially responsible behavior from brands. Social media marketing will involve aligning with causes, promoting sustainability, and engaging in purpose-driven initiatives. Brands that authentically demonstrate social responsibility and contribute to positive change will likely have an advantage in the future.

Overall, the future of social media marketing will revolve around personalization, video content, immersive technologies, social commerce, privacy, AI, and social responsibility. Marketers who stay ahead of these trends and adapt their strategies accordingly will be well-positioned to succeed in the ever-evolving social media landscape.

14.2   Emerging Technologies and Platforms

Emerging technologies and platforms refer to the new and innovative solutions that are entering the market or gaining traction in various industries. These technologies and platforms often have the potential to disrupt traditional methods and bring about significant changes in how businesses operate and individuals interact with technology. Here are a few examples of emerging technologies and platforms:

- **Artificial Intelligence (AI):** AI involves the development of computer systems capable of performing tasks that typically require human intelligence, such as visual perception, speech recognition, and decision-making.

AI has applications in various fields, including healthcare, finance, autonomous vehicles, and customer service.

- **Internet of Things (IoT):** IoT refers to the network of physical devices embedded with sensors, software, and connectivity to exchange data over the internet. It enables devices to collect and share information, leading to improved efficiency, automation, and convenience. IoT applications range from smart homes and cities to industrial automation and agriculture.

- **Blockchain:** Blockchain is a decentralized and distributed ledger technology that enables secure and transparent transactions across multiple parties. It provides a tamper-resistant record of transactions and eliminates the need for intermediaries. Blockchain has gained attention primarily in the financial industry for applications such as cryptocurrencies, smart contracts, and supply chain management.

- **Augmented Reality (AR) and Virtual Reality (VR):** AR overlays digital information onto the real world, while VR immerses users in a simulated environment. Both AR and VR have applications in gaming, entertainment, education, and training. They are also increasingly used in areas such as architecture, healthcare, and marketing.

- **5G Technology:** 5G is the fifth generation of wireless technology, offering significantly faster speeds, lower latency, and increased capacity compared to its predecessors. It enables the development of advanced applications such as autonomous vehicles, remote surgery, and smart cities.

- **Edge Computing:** Edge computing involves processing data near the source or at the edge of the network, rather than relying on centralized cloud computing. It reduces latency, improves real-time processing capabilities, and enhances data security. Edge computing is particularly beneficial for applications requiring quick response times, such as autonomous vehicles and Internet of Things devices.

- **Quantum Computing:** Quantum computing leverages quantum mechanical phenomena to perform computations that traditional computers cannot handle efficiently. It has the potential to solve complex problems in various domains, including cryptography, optimization, drug discovery, and weather forecasting.

These are just a few examples of the many emerging technologies and platforms that are shaping the future. As technology continues to evolve, new and exciting innovations are constantly being developed, offering transformative possibilities for businesses and society as a whole.

14.3　Continuous Learning and Adaptation

Continuous learning and adaptation refer to the ongoing process of acquiring new knowledge, skills, and behaviors, and adjusting one's approach in response to changing circumstances or feedback. It involves being open to new information, seeking opportunities for growth, and making necessary changes to improve performance or achieve desired outcomes.

In various contexts, continuous learning and adaptation can be applied:

- **Personal Development:** Continuous learning is essential for personal growth and development. It involves actively seeking new knowledge, exploring different perspectives, and acquiring new skills or competencies. By adapting to new information and experiences, individuals can enhance their abilities, broaden their understanding, and improve their overall effectiveness.

- **Professional Development**: In the workplace, continuous learning and adaptation are crucial for staying relevant and thriving in rapidly evolving industries. It involves keeping up with industry trends, advancements in technology, and best practices. Professionals need to continuously upgrade their skills and knowledge to meet changing demands, remain competitive, and take advantage of new opportunities.

- **Organizational Learning**: Organizations that foster a culture of continuous learning and adaptation are better equipped to navigate uncertain and dynamic environments. This involves promoting a growth mindset, encouraging employees to explore new ideas, and creating channels for sharing knowledge and feedback. By embracing change and learning from successes and failures, organizations can improve their performance, innovate, and adapt to market changes.

- **Artificial Intelligence and Machine Learning:** Continuous learning and adaptation are fundamental concepts in the field of artificial intelligence (AI) and machine learning (ML). Algorithms and models are designed to learn from data and continuously update their understanding to make accurate predictions or take appropriate actions. Adaptive systems can adjust their behavior based on feedback, allowing them to improve over time and handle evolving scenarios.

- **Decision-Making and Problem-Solving:** Continuous learning and adaptation are beneficial in decision-making and problem-solving processes. By actively seeking new information, considering different perspectives, and remaining open to feedback, individuals can make more informed decisions and find innovative solutions. Adapting one's approach based on new insights or changing circumstances increases the likelihood of achieving desired outcomes.

Overall, continuous learning and adaptation are critical for personal, professional, and organizational growth. By embracing a mindset of lifelong learning, individuals and organizations can stay agile, remain relevant, and effectively respond to the challenges and opportunities presented by a rapidly changing world.

CONCLUSION

In conclusion, "Amplify Your Brand: Mastering Social Media Marketing for Rapid Growth" is a comprehensive guide that unlocks the power of social media to propel your brand to new heights. Throughout this book, we have explored the ever-changing landscape of social media marketing and provided valuable insights, strategies, and tactics to help you navigate this dynamic realm with confidence and proficiency.

We began by emphasizing the importance of building a strong brand foundation and aligning it with your social media presence. We discussed the significance of identifying your target audience, defining your brand voice, and creating a cohesive visual identity that resonates with your followers. By doing so, you establish a consistent and recognizable brand that captures attention in the crowded digital space.

Furthermore, we delved into the various social media platforms and their unique features, allowing you to tailor your marketing efforts to reach your specific audience effectively. From Facebook to Instagram, Twitter to LinkedIn, and beyond, we explored how each platform operates and shared best practices for engaging your audience, creating compelling content, and utilizing paid advertising to maximize your brand's visibility and impact.

Throughout the book, we emphasized the importance of storytelling and authenticity in connecting with your audience. By sharing your brand's narrative, values, and purpose, you cultivate a loyal following who not only supports your products or services but also becomes advocates for your brand.

In addition, we discussed the power of influencer marketing and collaboration, showcasing how strategic partnerships can amplify your brand's reach and generate meaningful engagement. By leveraging the influence of others in your industry, you can tap into their established networks and leverage their credibility to build trust and expand your brand's reach.

We also explored the world of analytics and data-driven decision-making, providing you with the tools and insights to measure your social media performance, track key metrics, and adjust your strategies accordingly. By analyzing the data, you can identify what works, what doesn't, and continuously optimize your social media marketing efforts to achieve rapid growth and tangible results.

Ultimately, "Amplify Your Brand" serves as a roadmap to mastering social media marketing and harnessing its immense potential to fuel the rapid growth of your brand. By implementing the strategies and techniques outlined in this book, you will be equipped with the knowledge and skills to navigate the ever-evolving social media landscape, connect with your target audience on a deeper level, and position your brand for long-term success.

So, whether you are an entrepreneur, marketer, or business owner, this book empowers you to unlock the full potential of social media, amplify your brand's presence, and create a lasting impact in today's digital age. Embrace the power of social media marketing and set your brand on a trajectory of rapid growth. The future awaits, and it's time to amplify your brand like never before.

ABOUT THE AUTHOR

Seth N. Taylor is a highly accomplished success coach and a prominent figure in the world of entrepreneurship. With an unwavering passion for personal development and a keen business acumen, Taylor has carved a remarkable path for himself and inspired countless individuals to unlock their true potential.

Born and raised in a small town, Taylor's journey to success was not without its fair share of challenges. Growing up, he faced financial hardships and limited opportunities, which fueled his determination to create a better life for himself and others. Armed with a relentless drive and a thirst for knowledge, he embarked on a journey of self-discovery and personal growth.

Taylor's early years were marked by various entrepreneurial ventures, where he honed his skills and gained valuable experience in business management. Through both successes and failures, he cultivated a deep understanding of the intricacies of entrepreneurship, ultimately transforming his insights into a powerful coaching methodology.

Driven by his desire to uplift and empower individuals, Taylor made it his mission to help others overcome obstacles and achieve their goals. He delved into the world of personal development, studying psychology, mindset strategies, and leadership principles. Combining his practical experience as an entrepreneur with his expertise in personal growth, he developed a unique coaching approach that encompasses both business strategies and personal transformation.

As a success coach, Taylor has guided countless individuals, from aspiring entrepreneurs to seasoned professionals, in achieving their dreams. He empowers his clients to identify their true passions, break through limiting beliefs, and create a roadmap for success. His coaching style is marked by a compassionate yet no-nonsense approach, fostering an environment of accountability and growth.

Taylor's impact extends beyond his one-on-one coaching sessions. He is a sought-after speaker and has delivered inspiring talks and workshops on various platforms. His ability to captivate audiences and deliver actionable insights has made him a respected figure in the personal development and entrepreneurial communities.

In addition to his coaching endeavors, Taylor is also a successful entrepreneur himself. He has founded and scaled multiple businesses, demonstrating his ability to translate his knowledge and expertise into tangible success stories. His entrepreneurial ventures span diverse industries, from technology startups to real estate investments, showcasing his versatility and adaptability in the business world.

Today, Seth N. Taylor continues to be a guiding light for individuals seeking personal and professional transformation. Through his coaching, writing, and speaking engagements, he inspires others to embrace their full potential, break free from limitations, and create lives of purpose and fulfillment. With a relentless commitment to empowering others, Taylor is leaving an indelible mark on the world, one person at a time.